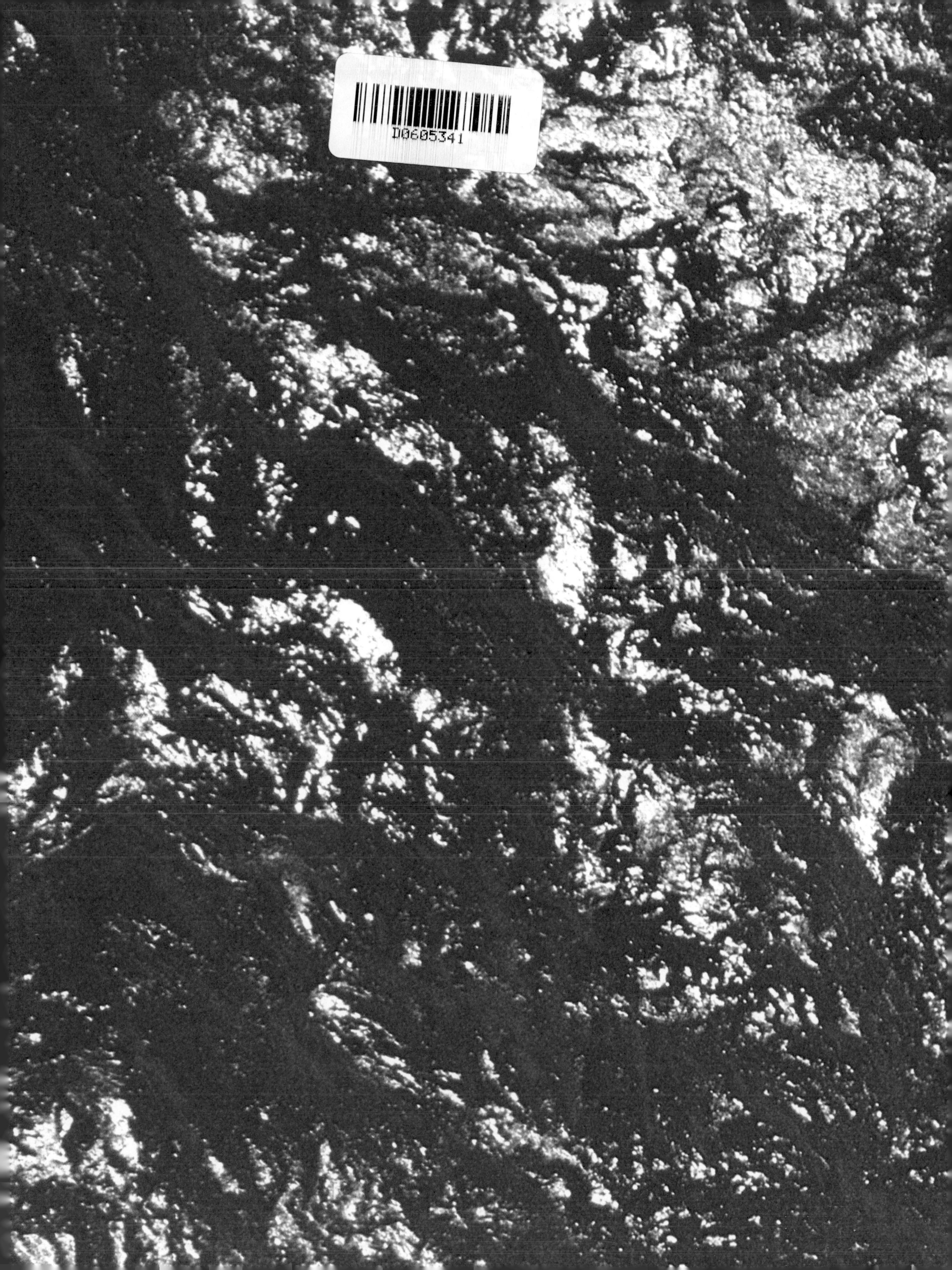

The Story of
SAIL

The Story of SAIL

Colin Martin · Norman Brouwer

WELDON
PUBLISHING

VOYAGES BEYOND THE GRAVE and
FIGHTING SAIL were written by
Dr Colin J.M. Martin
of the Scottish Institute of Maritime Studies,
University of St Andrews, Fyfe, Scotland

THE GOLDEN AGE OF SAIL was written by
Norman Brouwer
of the South Street Seaport Museum
New York

A Kevin Weldon Production
Published by Weldon Publishing
a division of Kevin Weldon and Associates Pty Limited
Level 5, 70 George Street Sydney, NSW 2000, Australia

First published in 1992

© Copyright: Kevin Weldon and Associates Pty Limited 1992
© Copyright design: Kevin Weldon and Associates Pty Limited 1992

Designed by Ray Harrington from an idea by Greg Meek
Typeset by Savage Typesetters, Brisbane, and
Amazing Faces, Sydney, Australia
Printed by Kyodo Printing Co, Singapore

Australian National Library Cataloguing-in-Publication data:

Martin, Colin, 1939-.
        The Story of sail.

        Includes index.
        ISBN 1 86302 239 2.

        1. Sailing ships – History. I. Brouwer, Norman J. II Title.

387.2043

CONTENTS

Contents

VOYAGES BEYOND THE GRAVE   6

   SUTTON HOO
   The Ship beneath the Meadow   8

   THE OSEBERG SHIP
   Grave of a Viking princess   16

FIGHTING SAIL   24

   MARY ROSE
   A sixteenth-century battleship in the Solent   26

   THE WARSHIP *WASA*   40

   HMS *VICTORY*
   "England expects..."   50

THE GOLDEN AGE OF SAIL   60

   BATAVIA
   The ill-fated East Indiaman   62

   CUTTY SARK
   In honour of a dancing witch   74

   PREUSSEN
   The "Pride of Prussia"   88

   SOBRAON
   The largest of her kind   98

ACKNOWLEDGEMENTS   110

INDEX   110

VOYAGES BEYOND THE GRAVE

To the ancients, death was a journey to Hades and sunless Cimmeria across the sinister and mysterious rivers of the lower world. Charon, the aged ferryman who for a coin (often placed in the mouth of the deceased) took souls on that final crossing, exemplifies the widely held concept of death as a passage over water. This was clearly the expectation of a humble Bronze Age fisherman in Fife, Scotland, who some 3,000 years ago was buried beneath his leather-covered coracle on a hillside overlooking the estuarine waters where he had once cast his nets. In just the same way, Cheops, the mighty pharaoh of Egypt, expected to circle the world for ever in the "Day and Night" boats which were buried, dismantled, in stone-lined pits at the foot of his Great Pyramid.

Nowhere was boat-burial more widespread than in northern Europe between about A.D. 400 and the coming of Christianity. This was an age of migration and warfare, of mighty deeds and grim tragedy. Ancient sagas, handed down by word of mouth until they were preserved by scribes in the Middle Ages, tell of how the heroic dead were laid to rest in their ships, to be buried, cremated, or set adrift (sometimes in flames) on the ocean.

Archaeologists have discovered more than 400 such burials, stretching from Brittany, through the British Isles, to Scandinavia and Iceland. Often, when the boat was burned during the burial ritual, all that remains is a scattering of iron nails or rivets that traces out the approximate shape of the vanished hull. Sometimes, if the boat was buried intact, the rivets survive in their original locations even though the wood of the hull may have rotted entirely away. In these cases skilled archaeologists are able to piece together the exact shape of the original craft. In very rare instances, fortuitous environments have preserved the wood of the ships, sometimes in miraculous condition.

Such practices have left us with a rich heritage of information about the ships of the Anglo-Saxon and Viking periods — periods of great importance in the development of maritime technologies. The pressures of those unstable times forced peoples on the edges of continental Europe to take to the seas, to raid, trade with, and ultimately to colonize the islands of the North Atlantic. In the tenth century, they reached the mainland of North America where, however, they remained only briefly. Ships were the tools with which these Dark Age seafarers performed their formidable deeds, and in striving ever to improve the performance and capabilities of their vessels they achieved a perfection of form that has never been surpassed.

FAR LEFT: Brass and enamel decoration on the so-called "Buddha bucket" (see page 21) unearthed with an ancient Viking ship.

LEFT: Carving from a wagon found with the same vessel.

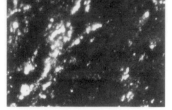

Sutton Hoo

8
–

The reconstructed helmet of
the ancient king, found in
his ship buried at
Sutton Hoo in East Anglia.

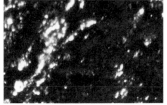

SUTTON HOO:

THE SHIP BENEATH THE MEADOW

The dead king's men had dragged the great ship a mile or more from the water's edge to the royal burial ground on the crags above the headwaters of the estuary. She was a magnificent open rowing vessel without a mast, 90 feet long from her elegantly curving prow to the tip of her matching stern. There were places for 40 oarsmen, and on the starboard side of the high stern a big steering paddle was lashed. The hull was built in the north-west European fashion of overlapping planks clenched with iron rivets, and the ship had seen long service afloat; a shipwright's eye might have discerned neat patches set into some of the planks. The voyage upon which she was embarking now was to be her final one.

But it was a voyage intended to last forever. She was to be the death ship of a pagan Anglo-Saxon monarch — possibly Raedwald, king of the East Angles and high king amongst the English, who died about A.D. 625. A great pit had been prepared for the vessel, and into this she was lowered. Though no trace of a body was found when the burial was excavated thirteen centuries later, it is possible that the acid soil had removed all evidence of it. At any event, the ritual that followed involved the disposition of the accoutrements and symbols of the dead king's power.

The king (whether or not his body was actually there) was arrayed for war. Within a specially constructed chamber in the center of the ship his personal equipment and weaponry were laid out — helmet, coat of mail, shield, sword and sword-belt, battleaxe, spears, and javelins. The helmet was a triumph of craftsmanship and artistic skill. It consisted of a forged iron cap with earflaps, neckguard, and full face mask. Its entire surface was embellished with sheets of tinned-bronze foil, stamped with decorative motifs, while the bronze crest, nose, moustache, and eyebrows combined to represent a flying bird. Zoomorphic symbols also adorned the great round shield. They included a stylized gilt-bronze dragon and a bird of prey, each richly decorated with interlaced designs studded with garnets, set on either side of an ornate central boss. The iron sword was pattern-welded — a costly and difficult technique which would have given the blade an appearance and temper fit for a great king — and was mounted with gold and garnet fittings, as were its accompanying scabbard and sword belt.

Among the items connected with the royal regalia were an enigmatic wrought-iron construction — perhaps a standard that was carried before the king in processions — and even more curious, a highly ornate whetstone. The king's personal accessories were no less splendid. They included gold shoulder-clasps, a huge and magnificent gold buckle, elaborate strap-mounts, and a gold-framed purse set with richly decorated plaques of gold, garnet, and

The great gold buckle that held the belt from which the king's purse hung (see page 14, the photograph of the objects in the earth where they were found).

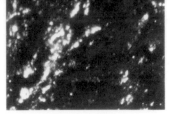

A modern reconstruction of the fragmentary lyre found in the grave.

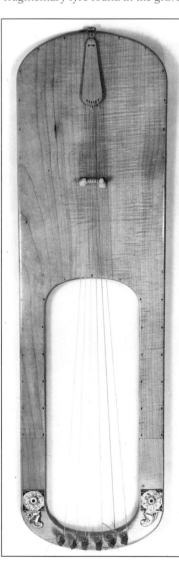

millefiori. The purse contained 37 small gold coins, all minted in Merovingian Gaul between 575 and 625, together with three unstruck gold blanks and two small ingots. Perhaps the coins were to pay the 40 ghostly rowers, and the ingots for a steersman, on the king's crossing into the afterlife.

Other objects piled into the burial chamber were associated with cooking and feasting. These included an iron-bound wooden tub and three buckets, three bronze hanging bowls, and three bronze cauldrons with iron suspension rings. Beside the largest of these, which measured 27 inches across and had a capacity of about twenty gallons, was placed the magnificently ornate iron chain, more than eleven feet long, which would have been used to hang the cauldron from a crossbeam in the king's timber feasting hall. His lavish lifestyle and the splendor of the hospitality at his court were reflected in the drinking horns, wood and ceramic bottles, and silverware that were buried with him. They probably contained food and drink for his final journey. Of the silverware, the most splendid was a great dish stamped with the control marks of the Byzantine emperor Anastasius I (A.D. 491–518).

The concern of the dead king's subjects to equip him for fighting and feasting in a pagan afterlife may not altogether have reflected his beliefs. Raedwald, the grave's most likely occupant, had briefly converted to Christianity during a visit to the neighboring kingdom of Kent, though he reverted to paganism on his return to East Anglia. Two silver spoons from the grave, inscribed with the names Saul and Paul in Greek letters, hint at an association with conversion and baptism that was quite at odds with the overt paganism of the other burial goods.

A final touch in equipping the king for his voyage beyond the grave was the provision, inside one of the large bronze bowls, of a six-stringed lyre. To the accompaniment of similar instruments, no doubt, bards would later sing songs, now long forgotten, describing the dead hero's achievements — and perhaps his magnificent funeral.

One description of the burial rites of a pagan king has, however, come down to us in the eighth-century English epic *Beowulf*. These rites may have been similar to those performed for the East Anglian king a century earlier. The story begins with the funeral of a Danish king, Scyld:

> . . . they laid their dear lord, the giver of rings, deep within the ship, by the mast in majesty; many treasures and adornments from far and wide were gathered there. I have never seen a ship equipped more handsomely with weapons and war-gear, swords and corslets; on his breast lay countless treasures that were to travel far with him into the waves' domain . . . Mighty men beneath the heavens, rulers in the hall, cannot say who received that cargo.

The East Anglian ship and its cargo of kingly splendor lay buried in the royal cemetery for more than thirteen centuries. When the funeral ceremonies were complete a great mound was piled over it and in time the barrow, and others surrounding it in the meadow of Sutton Hoo above the Deben estuary,

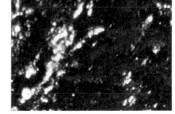

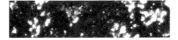

The Sutton Hoo ship, revealed by its carefully excavated impression in the sand. The rows of corroded iron rivets which joined the planks are clearly seen.

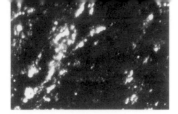

became part of the Suffolk landscape, covered in a grassy sward and all but forgotten. Once, perhaps in the sixteenth or seventeenth century, treasure-seekers dug into the mound, leaving behind fragments of a stoneware jar as evidence of their activities. Fortunately the burial chamber did not lie under the center of the mound, and so the robbers missed the royal treasure.

In 1938 Mrs Edith Pretty, owner of the Sutton Hoo estate, decided to investigate the ancient mounds. The work was entrusted to Basil Brown, a local archaeologist, who in that year opened three of the smaller mounds, only to find that each had been extensively robbed. But he did make two important discoveries. Enough had been left by the grave-robbers to show that the cemetery contained Anglo-Saxon burials of high status, and that one of them had once contained a boat. Although the wood had entirely rotted away, the twenty-foot vessel had left, not only its impression in the sand, but also the telltale iron rivets which had once fastened its planks. The stage was now set for a far greater discovery.

Brown's work in the Anglo-Saxon cemetery resumed in the summer of 1939, when war clouds were gathering over Europe. Mrs Pretty herself selected the mound to be investigated, choosing the largest — one which Brown had earlier rejected, considering it to have been disturbed in the past and therefore probably, like the others, robbed of its contents. Helped by John Jacobs, one of Mrs Pretty's gardeners, and her gamekeeper, William Spooner, Brown began to dig a trench through the center of the mound. Three days later Jacobs uncovered a row of iron rivets, their heads pressed firm against a hardened crust of sand, and Brown realized that he had found another boat. Within a few hours one of its upcurving ends had been revealed as a wonderfully clear impression in the sand, its plank runs sharply defined by the rows of rivets.

Jacobs and Spooner were set to wheelbarrowing away the spoil while Brown worked backwards into the ship, painstakingly revealing the rivet stains one by one but leaving a thin layer of sand to protect the fragile impression of the hull.

BELOW RIGHT: The fittings of the purse, reassembled on a modern lid. The lower half contains four plaques, those on the outside depicting men apparently being devoured by wolflike animals, and those in the centre showing birds of prey attacking their victims.

BELOW LEFT: A gold and garnet shoulder clasp, perhaps used to fasten the king's leather cuirass.

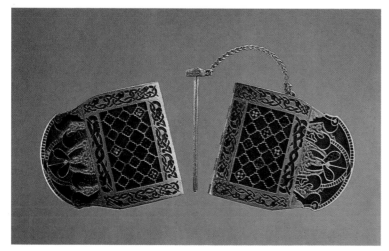

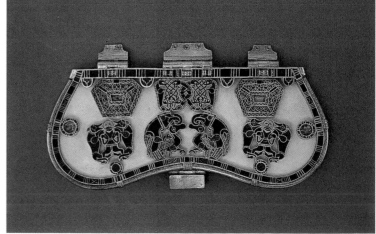

The function of the highly ornate whetstone that formed part of the royal regalia at Sutton Hoo is not entirely clear. It is certainly a magnificent item, with its four carved heads surmounted by a superb bronze stag mounted on an iron ring. Perhaps it was the King's scepter, and symbolized the mystical power of sharpening blades.

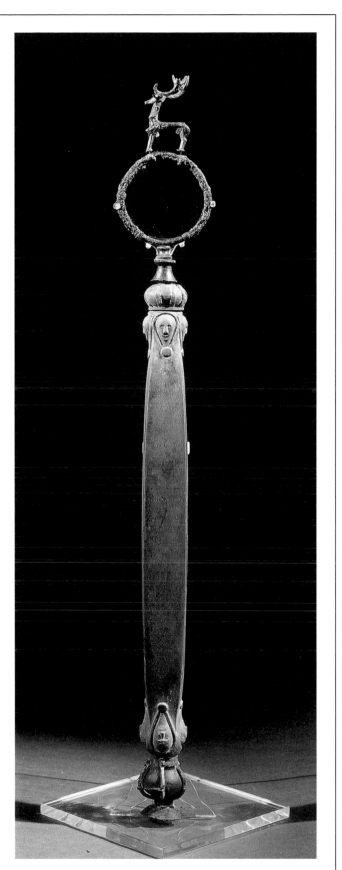

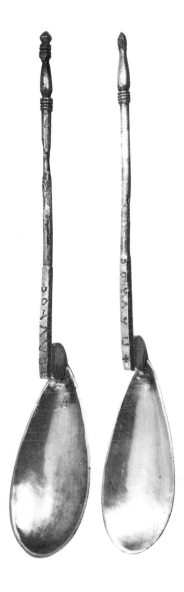

ABOVE: A pair of silver spoons, one inscribed in Greek with the name "Paul", the other "Saul". They may possibly relate to a Christian conversion by the king at some point in his life, though his burial was unquestionably pagan.

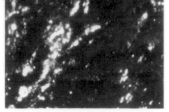

BELOW: The purse, coins, buckle, and mounts from the sword belt, revealed during excavation.

At first he expected the vessel to be a twenty-footer, like the one he had uncovered the previous summer, but as he worked along its length he realized, as its breadth continued to increase, that he was dealing with something much larger. By the time he had cleared 40 feet the width had reached nearly fifteen feet, and it had become apparent that his boat was a great ship, perhaps as much as 100 feet in length. About this time he came upon the pit dug by the would-be-grave-robbers, finding at its bottom broken fragments of the stoneware jar and the remains of a fire. From what he now knew of the ship Brown began to suspect that the robbers had missed its center and that the burial deposit, against all the odds, might still lie intact.

But more pressing problems were now presenting themselves. The excavation was now so deep that the trench needed to be widened to avoid the possibility of collapse. The growing likelihood of an undisturbed burial, too, demanded resources and skills which Basil Brown — though an experienced and extremely competent excavator — could not supply on his own. On 6 June a distinguished Cambridge archaeologist, Charles Phillips, visited the site, and at once recognized it as a discovery of supreme importance. Brown was asked to continue with his excavation of the ship, but the now positively identified burial area amidships, still untouched within its isolated block of soil, was to be left strictly alone.

On 10 July Phillips arrived to take charge on behalf of the Office of Works, as the find was now deemed to be one of national significance. Working with the indefatigable Brown and another local man, he spent a week carefully clearing away the sand which lay over the burial deposit. Shortly afterwards the team was joined by other leading archaeologists for the crucial and difficult operation of recording and lifting the treasure, much of which appeared to be contained in corroded and extremely fragile lumps. This was accomplished with skill and dispatch under great pressure of time, for it was now August 1939 and the impending world war, with all its dangers and uncertainties, was very close.

Not least of the excavators' difficulties was a lack of specialized equipment and resources, and a constant fear that the site — despite the care that had been taken not to publicize the find — might be raided by treasure-seekers. Policemen from the nearby town of Woodbridge mounted a discreet guard. The valuable objects were taken in charge by Mrs Pretty who, finding her safe too small to contain them, placed them under her bed. Much of the material, however, required urgent conservation treatment, and was rushed to London packed in newspapers or wet moss gathered from a plantation next to the site.

An inquest at Sutton Village Hall on 14 August ruled that because the treasure had been deposited in the ground as a deliberate act it was the property of the landowner, Mrs Pretty. Five days later, in an act of supreme generosity and wisdom, this remarkable lady donated the entire find to the nation. It is now one of the most important and popular exhibits in the British Museum.

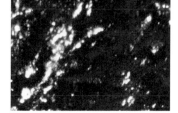

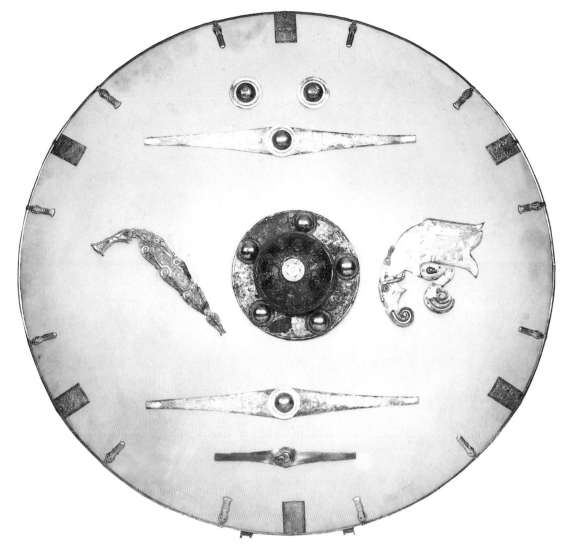

But what of the great royal ship, which had survived only as a ghostly impression in Sutton Hoo's sandy subsoil? Charles Phillips and his team, following the techniques pioneered by Basil Brown, carefully uncovered its shape and the lines of clenched fastenings which revealed the run of its planks. Even the internal ribs could be recognized as faint impressions in the sand, while along the gunwales the thorn-shaped tholes against which the king's oarsmen had once worked their looms showed as faint, but clear, discolorations in the soil. By a careful recording of such details the lost ship was brought to life on paper as a unique representation of a seventh-century East Anglian royal barge. Perhaps she was the very ship on which Raedwald had sailed to Kent to visit the court of King Aethelbert — and to become, albeit briefly, a Christian.

The war did not treat the ship's impression kindly. Though filled with bracken for protection, the hollow through the mound was frequently disturbed by military vehicles on training exercises, and the fragile remains became seriously degraded. Between 1965 and 1967 the site was re-excavated, and further details recorded before a plaster cast was taken of what survived. That cast is now in the British Museum with the treasures of the burial vault. In a sense, then, the dead king has been reunited with his ship.

ABOVE LEFT. A reconstruction of the king's shield.

BELOW: Stave-built bucket (the wood is modern) with iron fittings. It probably contained food or drink for the dead king.

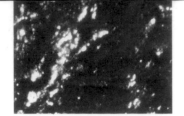

The restored Oseberg ship in the Viking Ship Museum, Oslo.

THE OSEBERG SHIP:
GRAVE OF A VIKING PRINCESS

Nothing can adequately prepare visitors for their first sight of the Oseberg ship. The deep brown oaken hull completely fills a vaulted gallery in the Viking Ship Museum outside Oslo, its long flowing lines combining classic simplicity with a breathtaking complexity of form. As the viewer walks round the ship its shape and perspectives constantly change in a harmony of shifting curves and fluent carpentry. This 1,200-year-old vessel, miraculously recovered and restored in the twentieth century, embodies much of the culture, achievements, and aspirations of the Viking age.

The ship, 71 feet long with a beam of seventeen feet, was built according to the "shell-first" clinker technique; that is, the overlapped planking was built up from the keel until the shape of the hull was realized, and only then were internal strengthening components added. By adjusting the width and set of the planks along their length the shipwright was able to exercise a subtle control over the shape of the hull as it grew upwards; the natural flexibility of the wood ensured that the three-dimensional geometry of compound curves achieved a natural harmony which no modern computer program could better.

The planks themselves helped in this process. They were not sawn from their parent log but split radially from it, so that the grain of each followed a constant warp-resistant pattern. Such planks were, in effect, tight bundles of grain, each fiber running along the entire length of the piece, quite unlike sawn planks where the grain pattern is variable and the individual fibers are frequently cut through.

Radially derived planks of this kind gave the Viking shipwright another advantage. When splitting them out of the log with wedges he could vary the thickness across each plank, and so achieve the edge-tapered cross-section demanded by the clinker technique. This allowed the tapering edges to be feathered together at the overlap prior to fastening with iron rivets. These were inserted every six inches or so, and clenched on the inside over a square washer or "rove."

An inevitable logic dictated the sequence of the Oseberg ship's construction. Its builder first set up the keel and curving extremities, taking the greatest care to ensure that they were true and square. He then built the plank runs upwards from the keel, merging each end smoothly into recesses cut into the stem and stern posts. Successive runs of planks were held temporarily in place until final checks and adjustments had been made, after which the rivets and roves were inserted along the overlapping join.

When the shipwright had completed nine runs, or "strakes," of planking along each side he began fitting the sixteen internal frames. Each had to be trimmed to an exact fit, because the shape of the hull was now unalterably

The vessels of the Norsemen were made with consummate skill. This view shows the intricate carving of the stern and the strong, over-lapping planks that formed the hull.

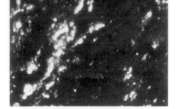

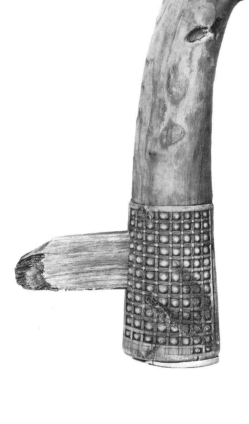

determined by the planked shell. These frames were lashed to cleats which had been left standing proud of the planks in the appropriate positions. Only the top strakes were left unlashed, being nailed to the upper parts of the frames.

At this point the two sides of the ship were tied together by transverse members — supported by short uprights — which linked the heads of the frames. These members carried a thick L-sectioned outer strake which gave the hull a distinct chine. This was the *meginhufr* (literally ''middle plank''), which provided lateral strength and allowed a smooth transition between the lower hull and the final two strakes. These in turn were supported by light standing knees set at the ends of the transverse members. The top strake, or gunwale, was pierced for fifteen oars along each side. Finally, the completed hull was trimmed by eye, to remove imperfections and smooth the curves.

This form of construction combined great strength with flexibility. The lower shell, though an integrally stressed structure, nevertheless preserved sufficient ''give'' to absorb the shifting loads on the hull as it moved through the water. Its pliability was enhanced by the spruce roots with which the frames were lashed to the strakes. But excessive twisting movements of the hull would have induced weaknesses, and it was to counter these that a more rigid structure was built above the *meginhufr*. In effect the hull consists of two ships, the lower flexible and sympathetic to changing stresses, and the upper providing complementary support.

A single mast was set amidships on a curved fish-shaped timber which spanned two of the frames. This was the *kerling*, or ''old woman,'' so named because of its stooped, hunchback appearance. A corresponding timber, or ''partner,'' secured the mast at the level of the transverse beams. On the Oseberg ship these elements appear to have been rather weak, since at some stage the partner had split and had been repaired and strengthened by the addition of two iron bands.

ABOVE: Carved animal head, probably part of a piece of furniture. This piece epitomises the skill and vigour of Viking art.

ABOVE RIGHT: A pair of boots from the Oseberg burial.

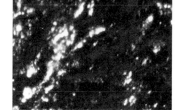

For all its elegance, this carpentry could have been carried out using only wedges, axes, augers and hammers, although it is probable that adzes, drawknives, planes and other basic cutting tools were also used. More sophisticated implements, however, would have been needed for the exquisite carving with which the Oseberg ship was adorned. Her high-curving prow and stern were solely for the purpose of embellishment, and this is richly supplied by friezes in deep relief of stylized animal figures, magnificently intertwined. Towards each end of the ship, where the gunwale begins its curve towards the vertical, beech-wood planks carry similar designs. Further carving is evident inside the prow.

Each extremity was finished in an exuberantly projecting spiral, more than sixteen feet above the keel, which ended in a serpent's or dragon's head. This symbolic mascot was intended to bring the ship luck and guide its sinuous hull through the water. The style of the carvings can be dated to about A.D. 800, which places the ship at the very beginning of the true Viking age.

Like the Sutton Hoo ship, this vessel was found in a burial mound. The farm of Oseberg lies on the western edge of the Oslo Fjord, in the ancient realm of Vestfold where the *Yngling* chieftains once held sway. In 1903 and 1904 the barrow was excavated by Professor Gabriel Gustafson, who found

The Oseberg ship where she was found, with her stern post and steering oar still in place.

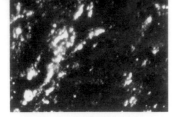

The Oseberg Ship

that it had been built of peat, which hermetically sealed its contents in the damp blue clay below. Because of this, the ship and its rich cargo of grave goods were almost perfectly preserved. The vessel pointed south, towards the sea, and was made fast by a hawser tied to a big rock near the bow.

The bow was packed with objects. There was a magnificent four-wheeled cart richly adorned with carving, three decorated sledges, three beds, a hand-loom, a small chair, two tents, the framework of a small shed, and various items of ship's equipment. Scattered among the mound, within and outside the ship, were the skeletons of thirteen horses, three dogs, and an ox. Most had been decapitated.

Near the center of the ship, just aft of the mast, was the main burial chamber. It was furnished as a bedroom, and in it lay the remains of two women. One had been aged about 65 and, when she died, had been suffering from almost complete disability caused by arthritis, palsy, and severe spinal inflammation. The other skeleton was that of a much younger woman, aged between 25 and 30. Their sepulcher had been richly equipped with beds, quilts, blankets, clothing and hung tapestries; by their sides, to keep them occupied during their voyage into eternity, provision had been made for the aristocratic womanly pastimes they had known in life — lamps, scissors, a cotton-box, blue dye, a linen-beater, and two looms. Conveniently to hand were supplies of food and drink, including a wooden bucket filled with wild apples which, when found, still preserved their flesh and peel intact.

Almost certainly the young woman had been of royal blood — perhaps she was Asa, one of the Vestfold queens. Her elderly companion is likely to have been a lifelong bondswoman or nurse, slain so that she could serve her mistress in the afterlife.

Cooking pot suspended from a collapsible tripod. This may have been a standard part of the ship's equipment, used in setting up camp during overnight stops ashore.

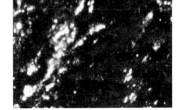

A magnificently ornate wooden cart from the Oseberg burial. It was probably used for ceremonial purposes.

OSEBERG RELICS

The stern of the Oseberg ship was found to be filled with many different kinds of domestic utensils. These included two cauldrons, axes, a kitchen stool, wooden dishes, ladles, knives, and a number of buckets. One of the buckets has been named the "Buddha bucket" because of its beautifully fashioned mounting, made of brass and enamel.

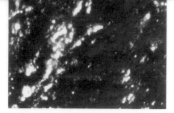

Another example of this grisly practice has been found in a Viking grave on the Isle of Man, where excavation revealed a dead warrior interred with his serving girl. Her skull still bears the terrible wound with which she was despatched before being buried with her master.

Even more harrowing to modern perceptions was the funeral of a Viking chief on the middle Volga about the year 921, described in chilling detail by an Arab diplomat, Ibn Fadlan. The ceremonies lasted more than a week and involved continuous ritual and feasting, intended to ensure the chieftain's swift passage to Valhalla.

A girl slave, having volunteered to die with her master, was treated with honor and reverence throughout the rites, in which she played the central role. Their climax was reached on the tenth day, when the dead man was brought from the place where he had lain in state to be dressed for burial and placed in a pavilion aboard his ship. Weapons, food, drink, and flowers were laid beside him, while his kinsmen erected their own pavilions around the funeral ship. A live dog was cut in two and its remains placed aboard the vessel, to be followed by the dismembered bodies of two horses, two cows, a rooster, and a hen.

The girl slave then visited the kinsmen's pavilions in turn, making love to each of them in honor of the dead man. Further ceremonies followed in which the girl, by this time mercifully intoxicated with ritual and wine, sacrificed a hen. Now she was taken in charge by two other girls and their old mother, known as the Angel of Death, who brought her aboard the ship and into the pavilion. Six of the chief's male relatives then made love to her again, in the presence of his body. They then laid her out beside the dead man and, holding her down, applied a garotte while the Angel of Death stabbed her repeatedly with a broad dagger. Finally the chieftain's closest relative, naked and walking backwards, applied a torch to the funeral pyre. The roaring flames, to the Viking mind, carried the chief and his devoted slavegirl straight to Paradise.

Though the Oseberg ship is thought to have been built about 800, the burial evidently took place much later — perhaps around 875. The ship seems to have been rescued from a semi-derelict state and refurbished for her funereal voyage. But she had always been something special. The elaborate carvings and supremely elegant lines mark the vessel as a royal pleasure craft, while her light structure and low freeboard show that she was designed, not for the open sea, but for the sheltered waters of the fjords. Nevertheless she is a supreme expression of the Viking shipwright's skill, combining a sense of beauty with a consummate understanding of the materials used in her construction.

Long after the queen had been buried the great mound at Oseberg, with its undertones of paganism and barbaric ritual, continued to exert a brooding influence over the flat boggy valley in which it stood. The excavators of 1903–04 found that they were not the first to have broken into the tomb. Earlier despoilers had entered the burial chamber and removed the greater part of the queen's skeleton, leaving that of her bondswoman intact. The royal beds, too, had been chopped in pieces, as if in a ritual act of killing.

Who had done this is a matter for speculation. Were they Christians, anxious to exorcise the power of a pagan past? Or were they superstitious locals, seeking to allay terrors which lay deep within their folk memory by annihilating the sinister spirits that dwelt in the great ship buried below the mound?

Weapons that were carried by Norsemen when the Oseberg ship sailed the seas.

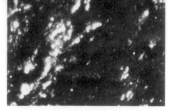

FIGHTING SAIL

 During the 1320s the first guns appeared in Europe, and they are recorded as being used — although they played a minor role — in 1340 at the sea battle of Sluys. In 1362 a Danish prince was slain by a *donnerbuchsen* (thunderbox) fired by a Lübeck ship, and so became the first recorded casualty of naval gunnery. But for nearly two centuries the shipboard gun remained more a curiosity than a serious weapon, although its capacity to frighten and disorient a foe was early recognized.

By the beginning of the sixteenth century, however, the potent combination of the sailing ship and the gun began to be exploited. This came about partly because ideas about sea warfare were changing, but more significantly because technical developments made the changes possible.

The earliest guns had been crude affairs, made up of strips of wrought iron welded together and reinforced with circular bands. Most were breech-loading. This gave them quite a high rate of fire but, because of the lack of a gas-tight seal between the chamber and the barrel, they were both short-range and extremely inaccurate. They were also for the most part small, and the few large ones that existed could not be used aboard ship because of the difficulty of absorbing their recoil.

During the second half of the fifteenth century bronze-founders perfected the technique of casting large gun barrels closed at the breech. Ballistically these muzzle-loading guns were much more efficient than the wrought-iron breech-loading types, and they were soon widely used on land to defend, or to besiege, castles and fortified towns. By the end of the century a number of European monarchs began putting them aboard their ships.

Ships too had been changing. For centuries sea warfare had been conducted by armies afloat, who regarded ships simply as vehicles to transport them to battle. A seaborne army was either landed close to an objective, or slugged it out with an adversary in a land-style battle. Ships became floating castles with high protective works designed to give military advantage to the soldiers aboard.

Such vessels reached their peak in the later fifteenth century with the development of the three-masted rig, which was devised primarily to improve the efficiency and cargo capacity of large merchant ships. The first naval three-masters were high-charged troop carriers *par excellence*, and such guns as they mounted were light supporting weapons only. But if problems of stability could be solved, and the structural difficulty of piercing the hull for ordnance overcome, ships of this kind would be capable of carrying the same heavy artillery that was proving so effective on land. By the early years of the sixteenth century these problems were being addressed, and the age of fighting sail had begun.

It is difficult to overstate the historical importance of the marriage between the sailing ship and the gun. The one employed the wind to achieve worldwide mobility; the other used gunpowder to apply concentrated and devastating force. Small numbers of men equipped with such tools could exercise decisive power anywhere in the world. For good or ill, three centuries of European global dominance had been made possible.

A carving of the royal coat of arms on the *Wasa*.

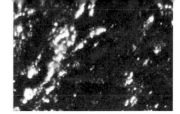

MARY ROSE:

A SIXTEENTH-CENTURY BATTLESHIP IN THE SOLENT

Lady Mary Carew stood on shore with the royal party, watching her husband's splendid warship *Mary Rose* turning towards the enemy. It was 19 July 1545, and two fleets were preparing for battle in the calm waters of the Solent, between the great English naval base of Portsmouth and the Isle of Wight. Bearing upon the eastern entrance to this narrow arena was a huge amphibious taskforce, carrying 30,000 invasion troops and commanded by the Admiral of France, Claude d'Annebault.

Waiting to oppose it were 60 ships belonging to the navy of Henry VIII, the English king, whose portly figure atop a warhorse dominated his field headquarters outside Southsea Castle. In his fleet's van was the flagship *Henry Grace a Dieu*, commanded by the admiral, Lord Lisle, who was closely supported by Vice-Admiral Sir George Carew in the *Mary Rose*. Hoisting their sails to catch the light summer airs the two royal ships began to get under way, bent on engaging the galleys which the French admiral had sent forward to probe the English defences.

At the start of her turn the *Mary Rose* had heeled unusually sharply to starboard as she caught the wind. This in itself was no great cause for concern, as the ship's natural stability could be expected to right her. But, inexplicably to the watchers on the shore, the ship continued to heel ever more steeply until her open gunports dipped below the water. The sudden ingress tipped the ship's balance beyond the point of no return, and in a matter of seconds she went down. King Henry, Lady Carew, and the others looked on in helpless disbelief as the *Mary Rose's* topmasts, with a handful of survivors clinging to them, emerged from the water. Of the 700 or so men on board only some 40 were saved, and among the dead was Sir George Carew.

LEFT: Henry VIII, King of England from 1509 to 1547. The *Mary Rose*, which was built in 1509 and lost in 1545, demonstrates many of the revolutionary changes in naval warfare which took place over that period.

RIGHT: A bronze Bastard Culverin, recovered from the sterncastle of the ship, mounted on replica gun carriage.

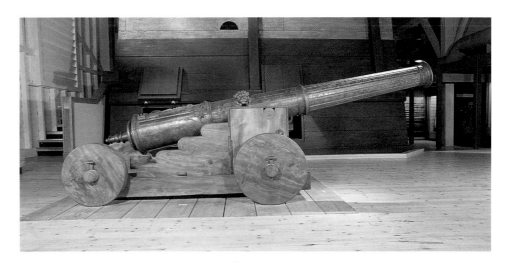

ſhiſe

Gonnepowder ſhotte · of · y

dij	Serpentyn powder in ʒarrellſ	ij laſt	ffor Cannon
ij ij			ffor ꝺ Cannon
ij	Corne powder in ʒarrellſ	iiij	ffor Culuerẏn
vj			ffor ꝺ Culuerẏn
			ffor Sakerſ

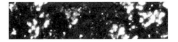

Mary Rose

ofte·of Stoey.
nd·Leade

porke peryb	cc	Bowes of yongg.	ccl
ffowlers	clxx	Boweftrynge	vj groc
toppe peryb	xx	Lyuer Arrowes	cccc
Bacffyb		in ffhibb	
He of leade	iiij c	Morryb pykeb	cl
Handgonneb	lx	Byllyb	cl
He of leade		Dartfforroppyb	xl

The *Mary Rose* as depicted by
Antony Antony in a Roll of 1546,
showing all the vessels of Henry
VIII's navy. In fact the ship had sunk
the year before, and while some of
the details shown by Antony have
been confirmed by the hull's
recovery there are discrepancies –
in particular, the Mary Rose was
of much sleeker build than the
illustration suggests.

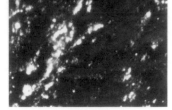

An eighteenth-century engraving of a contemporary painting (since destroyed) showing the sinking of the *Mary Rose* on 19 July 1545. On the left the leading French galleys enter the Solent as the English flagship *Henry Grace à Dieu* moves to intercept them. Towards the shore the topmasts of the capsized *Mary Rose*, with survivors clinging to them, protrude from the water. Outside Southsea Castle the portly mounted figure of Henry VIII can be seen.

THE ENCAMPMENT OF THE ENGLIS

TOGETHER WITH A VIEW OF THE ENGLISH AND FRENCH FLEETS AT T.

ENGRAVED FROM A COEVAL PAINTING AT COWDRY IN SUSSEX THE SE.

The cause of the disaster may never be known for certain. However, it is possible that the sheer weight of troops on the upper works and their lack of discipline — as the ship heeled Sir George is reported to have cried out, "I have the kind of fools I cannot rule" — unbalanced the *Mary Rose* at a crucial point in the turn.

This was the only serious casualty of a war that never happened. Shortly afterwards the French invaders, having briefly ravaged the Isle of Wight and made an ineffectual landing at Seaford, returned to Boulogne. In the Solent

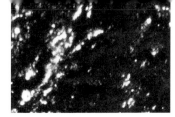

CES NEAR PORTSMOUTH,
NCEMENT OF THE ACTION BETWEEN THEM ON THE XIX.TH OF JULY MDXLV.
ONOURABLE ANTHONY BROWNE LORD VISCOUNT MONTAGUE

unsuccessful efforts were made to salvage the *Mary Rose*, whose remains there-
after lay forgotten for 291 years. Then, in 1836, the pioneer divers John and
Charles Deane, who were working on the wreck of a warship which sank off
Spithead in 1782, happened upon the *Mary Rose*. Over the next four years they
salvaged a number of objects, including four bronze guns, eleven pieces of
wrought-iron artillery, longbows, and some pottery. Everything else, they
noted, was deeply buried in the mud, and in 1840 they moved on. Henry
VIII's great battleship sank back into oblivion.

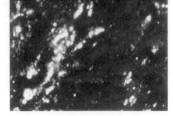

BELOW RIGHT: A selection of objects found inside the Barber Surgeon's cabin, including ceramic jars for medicine, a pewter bleeding bowl, a large barber's shaving bowl, canisters, a razor, a urethral syringe, plates and a large wooden mallet.

BELOW LEFT: Gimbaled ship's compass, one of the three recovered from the *Mary Rose.*

BELOW: A sailor's shoe from the *Mary Rose,* with a high vamp and slashed decoration.

In 1967 Alexander McKee, a diving historian who had launched a program to locate historic shipwrecks in the Solent, arranged with Professor Harold Egerton of the Massachusetts Institute of Technology to conduct a sonar survey over the area in which he suspected the *Mary Rose* lay. A seabed anomaly, consisting of a mound and down-tide scour pit, was identified and inspected by McKee and his divers who, however, found no visible remains. Three years later this anomaly was proved to be the actual wreck, when a shift of the surface sediments unexpectedly revealed the eroded tops of the ship's timbers.

It was a momentous discovery. If, as seemed likely, much of the ship and her contents had been preserved in the soft mud into which she had apparently sunk, the remains might be revealed and recovered by modern techniques of underwater archaeology. The way was clear for what would become the largest and most ambitious underwater excavation ever mounted in British waters.

The enormous historic importance of the wreck was recognized from the outset, and operations on it have been conducted with all the systematic care and thoroughness of an archaeological excavation on land. Under the guidance of Dr Margaret Rule, a practising archaeologist who learned to dive in order to direct the project, the site was surveyed and analyzed. An initial assessment, completed in 1978, showed that the major part of the ship's starboard side was encapsulated in the mud, heeled over at an angle of 60 degrees. It was therefore decided to excavate the ship and remove its contents for study, conservation, and display in a specially established museum at Portsmouth. The feasibility of raising and preserving the hull would then be considered.

From 1979 to 1982, when the excavation closed, 24,640 individual dives were made by the archaeological team and their corps of volunteer helpers, amounting in all to nine man-years on the seabed. Thousands of individual finds were recorded, raised, and conserved; loose timbers were removed and stored for later reconstruction within the hull; and the complex archaeology of the wreck was revealed and interpreted by careful dissection. At last, on 11 October 1982, in a dramatic operation that was watched live on television across the globe, the empty hull was successfully recovered.

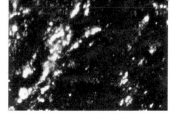

Through a continuing program of excavation, research, preservation, and display, the *Mary Rose* team has opened a fascinating window on the Tudor world. The ship and her people were frozen, as it were, at the very moment of disaster. The fatal ports were found still open, the bronze and iron muzzles of their guns ready to roar defiance at the French. The skeleton of an archer, recognizable by the bundle of arrows among his bones and by deformities to his spine and left forearm caused by years of wielding the longbow, lay where he had drowned. A chest containing the medicines and equipment of the ship's barber-surgeon stood in his cabin, ready for the grim business of tending the wounded once battle was joined.

Although the *Mary Rose* was old when she sank in 1545 — she was built at Portsmouth in 1509–10: she still represented the latest thinking in naval warfare. From the beginning she had been designed to carry artillery, with gunports cut low above the waterline to accommodate heavy guns. This was a revolutionary concept in 1509: although guns had been carried aboard warships for nearly 200 years they had up till then been small anti-personnel weapons, wielded from the upper decks and fighting tops. Although such weapons might cause light casualties and, with their noise and smoke, lower enemy morale, they rarely won battles. That could only be achieved by grappling an enemy ship and overwhelming it by military force, the simple tactic that had dominated naval warfare throughout the medieval period.

ABOVE LEFT: The hull of the *Mary Rose* at the surface of the Solent.

BELOW: In the murky waters of the Solent a diving archaeologist inspects the remains of the *Mary Rose*.

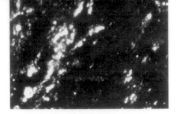

ABOVE: Adrian Barak, one of the project archaeologists, examines a yew longbow recovered from the wreck.

ABOVE RIGHT: The parrel asemblage, one of the most complex items of rigging recovered from the ship's stores on the orlop deck. Acting with a "ball bearing" type of action they allowed the yard to be hoisted up the mast and secured in position.

An ability to carry large loads was the prime requirement of medieval warships, which were generally adaptations of cargo vessels. Indeed they were often one and the same: in time of war kings often requisitioned private ships for naval use, while during peace the royal ships might be employed in lucrative commercial ventures. All that was needed to equip a vessel for fighting was to fit its bow and stern with raised "castleworks" to give the troops protected fighting platforms.

By the end of the fifteenth century the potential of guns for naval warfare was becoming recognized, and in 1495 Henry VII's new ship *Sovereign* mounted no fewer than 151 pieces of artillery. But they were very small and, following earlier practice, they were all mounted topsides. No one had yet considered piercing the hull so that heavy pieces could be mounted as a broadside along the main decks. Indeed, in the case of the *Sovereign* this would have been structurally impossible, because she had been built in the northern European fashion of overlapping clinker planks. To cut through them would have destroyed the ship's structural integrity.

Within fifteen years a revolution had taken place. In 1509 the *Sovereign* was completely rebuilt at Portsmouth. Her clinker planking was removed and replaced with butt-jointed, flush carvel strakes built on a strong internal skeleton, and she was given a brand-new armament of heavy guns. The rebuilt ship now mounted sixteen bronze muzzle-loading guns in place of her earlier light iron breech-loaders, and most of these must have been carried below decks, with gunports cut in the flush planking to accommodate them.

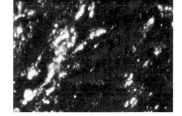

Later that year, in the same royal yard, the keels of two new warships were laid down — the *Peter Pomegranite* and the *Mary Rose*. By summer 1511 the *Mary Rose* was in the Thames fitting out (this included the issue of uniforms in Tudor green and white for some of her crew), and in 1512 she saw her first active service off the French coast. In 1521 a list of the king's ships recorded her tonnage as six hundred.

When the *Mary Rose* was 26 years old, in 1536, she was extensively rebuilt and uprated to 700 tons. What emerged was essentially a new ship. Her ability to mount heavy ordnance was massively increased by strengthening the interior of the hull with diagonal bracing (it was previously thought that this technique was not invented until the nineteenth century), and she was rearmed to match her new capacity.

The remains of the *Mary Rose's* hull undergoing conservation at Portsmouth. Most of the starboard side has survived.

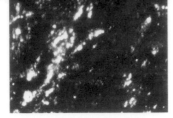

A collection of personal items including leather pouch, gold coins, rosary, whistle, clasp, thimble, ring, die, pocket sundial, seal and wooden comb.

For all these changes the ship retained the traditional role of a floating fortress packed with troops, and her castleworks, covered waist, and overhanging prow were clearly designed with soldiers in mind. Of these probably the most numerous — and certainly the most deadly — were archers: men trained from boyhood in the use of the yew longbow, who could cast a barrage of armor-piercing missiles from a range of 200 yards at a rate of up to six per minute. The boarding and capture of the adversary was still considered to be the aim of a successful sea fight, and the troops were provided with bills and pikes for close-quarter fighting. As discoveries from the wreck have shown, some men were also equipped with round wooden shields which had short handguns incorporated into their bosses.

But although shock troops were an essential part of the *Mary Rose's* fighting capacity, heavy guns were seen as equal partners. An inventory made about the time of her sinking records a total of fifteen bronze muzzle-loaders, ten of which have been recovered (four by the Deanes, and six during the recent excavations). The largest, of eight-and-a-half-inch bore, would have fired an iron shot of more than 60 pounds, while the average shot-weight of the other

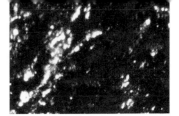

Mary Rose

The revolution in English shipbuilding of the early sixteenth century occurred, apparently, at the behest of the new king, Henry VIII, who came to the throne in 1509. It was in accordance with his ideas that the Sovereign was rebuilt, and it was in the year of his accession that the Mary Rose was begun.

The loss of the Mary Rose, 36 years later, was deeply felt by the king. As early as 1513 – long before she was upgraded – her commander, Sir Edward Howard, had described her to Henry as "the flower I trow of all ships that ever sailed". When, in 1545, she sailed to do battle with the French off Spithead, she embodied in every respect Henry VIII's state-of-the-art approach to naval warfare.

In some respects the naval technologies Henry had created were ahead of their time – no one yet knew how to use them effectively, and this may have contributed to the disaster. Yet the Mary Rose and her sisters embodied ideas which, 40 years later, would help to defeat the Spanish Armada. And Nelson's great ships-of-the-line which won the day at Trafalgar in 1805 could trace their line directly back to Henry's naval innovations.

nine was around 25 pounds apiece. Even allowing for the probability that some of the missing pieces were quite small, this represents an extremely heavy primary armament. Nor was it the ship's sole firepower. She also carried 24 heavy wrought-iron breech-loading pieces, 52 anti-personnel weapons, and 50 handguns for use at close quarters.

An analysis of the way in which this formidable weaponry was distributed and mounted aboard the ship makes it clear that the *Mary Rose's* armament represented a carefully considered and integrated weapons system. Seven guns were found in position along the starboard side of the main deck, most of them still on their wooden carriages. Together with the portside ordnance and chase pieces at bow and stern this lower battery consisted of up to eighteen pieces.

A watercolor illustration by the Deane brothers of bronze guns they raised from the wreck of the *Mary Rose* in 1836.

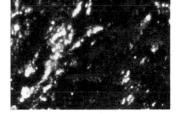

In these, the ship's heaviest guns, bronze alternated with iron. Normally they were secured behind lidded gunports, but they could be run out at a moment's notice to deliver ship-smashing broadsides at a range of up to 200 yards. The bronze guns were mounted on four-wheeled truck carriages, each tailor-made for its particular piece. Such carriages, of which the *Mary Rose* examples are the earliest known, were extremely efficient for use aboard ship. Their compact design allowed a gun muzzle to project well out of the port, while the rear part of the carriage scarcely extended beyond the breech. Sufficient room was therefore available to allow the gun to be hauled inboard for reloading.

Big guns were not confined entirely to the lower deck. A lighter, but nevertheless substantial, battery was carried on the upper and weather decks, while a ten-pounder culverin was found on the sterncastle deck, pointing forward. From there it could provide frontal fire as the ship approached an adversary, or sweep its own decks if boarders entered by the waist.

The ship, then, possessed a number of tactical options which could be deployed individually or in concert. She could fight a stand-off action, bombarding her adversary with heavy broadside artillery; when the range was sufficiently close a blanket fire of arrows could be added; and at closer ranges the smaller iron breech-loaders could be brought in to add to the confusion. Finally an enemy, thus softened up, could be boarded and carried by storm.

Similar tactical options were available to Lord Nelson when, aboard his flagship *Victory*, he faced the combined French and Spanish fleets off Cape Trafalgar in 1805. The age of fighting sail was to endure for more than 300 years.

The *Mary Rose* in No. 3 Dry Dock, on display in the controlled environment of the Ship Hall, Portsmouth.

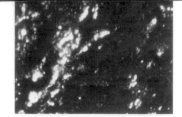

Wasa in dry dock in 1961.

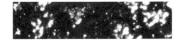

THE WARSHIP *WASA*

Naval warfare underwent radical changes in the sixteenth century, during which the sailing warship was transformed from a floating troop carrier to a mobile, hard-hitting artillery platform. The *Mary Rose* of 1545, with her massed archers and tall castleworks bristling with anti-personnel pieces complemented by heavy broadsides below decks, represented an intermediate stage in this process. Forty years later it was almost complete, as exemplified by the galleons with which Queen Elizabeth's navy successfully resisted the Spanish Armada's attempt to invade England in 1588.

These purpose-built fighting machines carried almost no soldiers. Spared the need to accommodate large bodies of fighting men, designers could dispense with the wind-catching castleworks at bow and stern and so improve the sailing performance of their ships. This was further enhanced by a more efficient sail plan and a longer, sleeker hull. Only one major problem of design remained — that of combining nimbleness with the capacity to carry an increasingly heavy armament.

Elizabethan shipwrights balanced this fine equation with a precision that bordered on genius. The underwater lines were refined according to what was to become the classic dictum "head of a cod and tail of a mackerel." This principle was shown graphically in a series of technical drawings, executed in about 1586 by the Queen's shipwright Matthew Baker. The new shape minimized water resistance without reducing the hull's stability, so that full advantage could be taken of the reduced topside weight by placing a much heavier armament on the main decks. The ship had become a mobile battery.

Now that the ship's fighting strength lay in guns rather than in soldiers, tactics changed accordingly. The object was no longer to close and board, but to use superior mobility and firepower to batter an adversary into submission. But this proved no easy task, and in the Armada conflict the new tactics resulted in a curious stalemate. The Spaniards, whose aim was not to defeat the English at sea but to land an invasion taskforce, stuck to the traditional approach of packing their ships with soldiers. Although these lumbering troop transports stood no chance of outmaneuvering the nimble gun platforms of their adversaries they nevertheless retained an almost unassailable defensive advantage, for if an English ship came too close it would be overwhelmed by the Spanish soldiers.

The result was an inconclusive sparring match. Guns on their own could not annihilate a disciplined formation like the Armada, and after the English ran out of ammunition the fleets disengaged with relatively little damage on either side. Bad Spanish planning and unseasonable weather, rather than the superiority of Elizabeth's galleons, were the roots of the Armada's ultimate downfall.

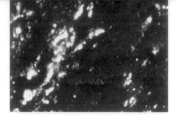

The Warship Wasa

4 2

The restored *Wasa* in her own
museum, Vasamuseet, in Stockholm.
The elaborate carving of the stern
castle can be seen clearly. Overall,
the ship has 700 pieces of carving on
the hull.

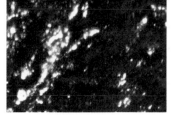

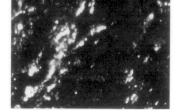

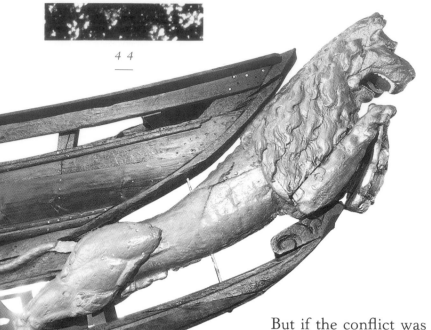

ABOVE: The *Wasa's* great lion figurehead alone weighs several tons. The weight of so much decorative sculpture above the waterline may have contributed to the disaster.

ABOVE RIGHT: One of *Wasa's* large bronze 24-pounders.

A sailor's chest was found on the upper gun deck, containing his personal belongings. This type of felt hat was quite common during the seventeenth century.

But if the conflict was inconclusive, experience gained by both sides had a profound effect on the development of fighting ships in the years to come. The mobile gun platform, suitably refined to remedy shortcomings revealed by the test of battle in 1588, became the basis of all future warships. Its potent combination of wind-generated mobility with the destructive energy of gunpowder forged a weapon which dominated European conflicts and global rivalries until the age of steam. And the mud of Stockholm harbor has preserved, in almost pristine condition, a superb example of such a ship.

In 1625 King Gustavus Adolphus of Sweden, alarmed at the German emperor's plans to build a fleet to invade Protestant Scandinavia, ordered the construction of four great warships. The ships would incorporate the very latest in naval technology, and their design and construction were entrusted to a Dutchman, Henrik Hybertsson. One of the two largest was to be called *Wasa* after the royal house. Her keel was laid at Stockholm in 1626, and the ship was launched the following year. In the spring of 1628 she was brought to the Royal Palace dockyard to receive ballast and armament, and on the fine Sunday afternoon of 10 August a multitude of excited people watched her embark upon her short maiden voyage. The king himself was away, campaigning in Poland.

As she warped downstream from the dockyard against a light south-southwest breeze *Wasa* must have presented a magnificent sight. With an overall length of 200 feet and a beam of 38 feet she displaced nearly 1400 tons and mounted an armament of 64 bronze guns. The 48 heaviest, each weighing one and a half tons and firing a 24-pound shot, were arrayed along the two main decks as continuous broadsides.

Her long hull was spendidly adorned with painted and gilded carvings. The huge lion figurehead, sheathed in gold leaf, symbolized the power and might of the crown. It weighed several tons. At the high stern were the crowned arms

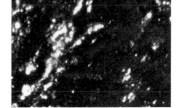

of the Wasa dynasty, supported by lions rampant. The quarter-galleries were richly decorated with further carvings — mermaids, warriors, cherubs, classical figures, grotesque masks, animals, and heraldic shields.

As *Wasa* reached the southern side of Stockholm harbor she turned eastwards to catch the breeze, setting her fore and main topsails, foresail, and mizzen. Her rig followed the pattern adopted by all large warships over the previous decade or so. The mainmast, raked backwards at an angle of some five degrees, carried three sails — main, top, and royal. The two topsails were set on topmasts which could be struck to reduce top hamper in bad weather. A similar arrangement was provided for the foremast. Aft, a single mizzen carried a lateen lower sail and a square topsail, while above the bowsprit and its spritsail a short mast — the spritsail topmast — bore a further sail, the spritsail topsail. Though no contemporary picture of *Wasa* exists, an identical rig can be seen in Conrad Visscher's engraving of a French naval vessel, built in Holland in 1626.

The lower gun deck of the *Wasa*. Her massive construction is evident. Empty carriages line the sides: the bronze 24-pounders once mounted on them were salvaged in the seventeenth century.

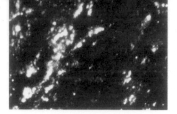

ABOVE: The ruling Swedish dynasty had a corn sheaf on their coat of arms, the word for corn sheaf (*vase*) being the derivation of the *Wasa*'s name.

ABOVE LEFT: Roof decoration from the port side of the lower gallery, in the form of a mermaid.

ABOVE RIGHT: Port side decorations at the stern of the *Wasa*.

Vespers had just struck in Stockholm's Great Church as *Wasa's* sails began to fill, setting her on a starboard tack across the harbor. As she approached the island of Beckhomen she was hit by a sudden squall, and, just as the *Mary Rose* had done 83 years earlier, began to heel alarmingly. Erik Jonsson, the chief gunnery officer, ran below to order the transfer of artillery to windward, but it was too late — water began to pour in through the lee gunports, and the ship was doomed. With all flags flying she went down in 110 feet of water, and many of the 200 or more people on board were drowned.

An enquiry into the cause of the sinking was inconclusive. Henrik Hybertsson, her builder, was dead, and since the king himself had passed the plans no direct criticisms were leveled. But it seems likely that a combination of factors caused the disaster. It was suggested that she may have been too narrow and too sharp in her bottom. She had perhaps taken on board insufficient ballast to counteract the weight of her artillery, which was greater than originally specified. Again, the weight of the elaborate — and in practical terms entirely superfluous — embellishments on her upper works was undoubtedly a contributory factor. Finally, the inexperience of the crew may explain their tardiness in taking remedial action.

Three days after the disaster an English engineer, Ian Bulmer, was given permission to salvage the ship but, although he managed to right the hull on the seabed, his attempt to raise it failed. Further efforts by Swedish divers the following year met with no success. In the 1660s, however, two salvage experts, Albrecht von Treileben and Andreas Peckell, managed to raise most of the ship's valuable bronze guns by hoisting them through the open ports. Dressed in flexible leather suits to protect them from the cold, they worked

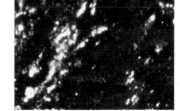

from a lead diving bell and looped lifting ropes round the gun muzzles by means of a six-foot boathook. With such primitive equipment the recovery of the guns, each of which weighed one and a half tons, from a depth of 110 feet in the cold and murky waters of Stockholm harbor was, to say the least, an impressive feat.

Once most of the guns were recovered there seemed little point in salvaging *Wasa's* now aging hull, and its resting place was soon forgotten. But in 1954 Anders Franzen, a Swedish amateur historian and archaeologist, began a systematic search for the ship. He knew that the low salinity of the Baltic was well suited to the preservation of wooden hulls, and he suspected that *Wasa* might still lie virtually intact at the bottom of the harbor.

With great ingenuity Franzen devised a simple tool to aid his search. It was a streamlined heavy metal "bomb," its nose fitted with a carpenter's wad punch which was designed to extract a small plug of whatever it hit. Month in, month out, he probed the bed of Stockholm harbor. Eventually, in the summer of 1956, he came upon an obstruction which yielded samples of black oak wherever he dropped his device. A Swedish navy diver was sent down to investigate, and on reaching the bottom he found himself standing at the foot of a great wooden wall that rose vertically from the seabed. It was the side of the *Wasa*.

Restored and unrestored gunports on the Wasa.

When each of the Wasa's gunport lids was raised it revealed the arresting image of a roaring golden lion's head, with bulging eyes and bared fangs, against a background of vivid red. It symbolized the destructive power of the gun whose muzzle protruded beneath it. To any foe who saw the tiers of ports snapping open in unison as the ship prepared for action, such symbolism would have been frighteningly explicit – as, of course, it was intended to be.

The broadside was now a vastly more potent weapon than it had been a century before, thanks to the standardization and mass-production of guns, and increased skill in using them.

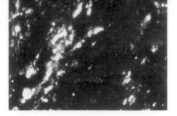

The elaborate stern decoration includes these two cherubs holding a coat-of-arms – the corn sheaf of the Wasa dynasty.

A huge recovery operation followed. Divers drove six tunnels underneath the hull, through which great steel wires were passed to form a lifting cradle. During this operation many thousands of objects were recovered from inside and around the wreck, including many of the elaborate carvings that had decorated the ship, particularly at the stern. Most had fallen from the hull when their iron fastenings had rotted and had been preserved undamaged in the soft mud.

At length the ship was eased from the muddy bed into which she had sunk, though she was not yet ready to surface. The fragile hull was first deposited in shallower water where divers could work to seal up the gunports, repair the damaged stern, and strengthen the weakened structure with steel bolts. Finally, on 24 April 1961, *Wasa* broke surface, and by 4 May was afloat on her own keel. Shortly after that her long-delayed voyage ended when she entered dry dock, less than half a mile from the berth she had left 333 years earlier.

Now *Wasa* is one of Stockholm's major attractions as a museum in her own right. The great hull, almost entirely restored and with its carved embellishments back in place, is naturally the central focus of the display. But a ship is much more than an empty hull. Complementary displays, based on material recovered during the long processes of excavation and preservation, provide unique glimpses of life on board a seventeenth-century warship. Carpenters' tools, rope and rigging, sails, a capstan, and even the ship's longboat, reflect the daily routines of life aboard. Food remains include corn, oats, peas, rye, wheat, fish, and meat. The meals would have been prepared in the great brick-lined galley set in the hold forward of the mainmast, and issued to the crew in the wood and pottery vessels which were found on the decks. Some of the sailors' clothing was also discovered, together with eighteen skeletons, two of them female.

More important than all this is the fact that *Wasa* survives exactly as she was built and equipped three and a half centuries ago — a priceless example of an early modern sailing warship. Compared with the ships that fought the Armada, or the *Mary Rose*, the most striking thing about her is the purposeful uniformity of the two gun decks which housed the four dozen 24-pounders of her main batteries. Most of the compact truck carriages remained in place, though without their guns; these had been salvaged by the redoubtable von Treileben and his divers. But three guns, including one of the main battery pieces, were left on the wreck.

This gun bears the royal arms of Gustavus Adolphus and has the standard six-inch bore of a 24-pounder. Its 47 vanished sisters were in all respects identical. This degree of standardization contrasts with the hotch-potch nature of the weaponry carried by the *Mary Rose*, and by both sides in the Armada campaign. The Spaniards in particular had suffered, not only because of the bewildering variety of types and sizes in the ordnance carried by their ships, but also because they had to contend with several quite different standards of weights and measures. This caused inefficiencies which made their artillery

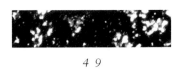
almost totally ineffective in the melee of a battle. The English, who relied on guns as their primary weapon at sea, had fared only marginally better.

In *Wasa*'s armament we see the beginnings of institutionalized naval technology, in which standardization and factory production replaced the idiosyncratic and administratively chaotic sixteenth-century approach to sea warfare. By the early seventeenth century the European maritime nations had devised a weapon which would change little over the following two centuries but which, with careful honing, would become a fighting machine with a destructive potential that its instigators could scarcely have imagined.

Elaborate decorations at the stern of the *Wasa*.

HMS Victory

5 1

HMS *VICTORY:*

"ENGLAND EXPECTS..."

The powder monkeys were teenage boys, some as young as twelve. Only they were allowed to pass by the grim-faced marine sentries on *Victory*'s three gun decks as they scurried back and forth on their ceaseless errand to bring cartridges filled with powder up from the magazines below the orlop deck. They were a part of the 850-strong team which allowed *Victory*'s 104 guns to fire at a best rate of once every 90 seconds. And this capacity — perhaps two or three times that of her French and Spanish adversaries' guns — paid the ultimate dividend off Cape Trafalgar on 21 October 1805.

There, close to Spain's southern tip, Napoleon's naval forces had finally been brought reluctantly to battle by the tenacious genius of the British admiral, Lord Nelson. Nelson's tactics for the coming engagement were simple and brilliantly unconventional. Instead of forming a line-of-battle to engage Admiral Villeneuve's Combined Fleet of 33 ships, spread out in a straggling column inshore of the British fleet as they sought the sanctuary of Cadiz, he divided his force of 27 sail into two line-astern groups. These would bear down on Villeneuve's line, smashing its center and precipitating a general melee in which Nelson knew that his fleet's superior discipline and firepower would prevail. Once battle was joined, victory would be determined by the spirit and fighting capacity of each crew, and everyone in the fleet knew it, thanks to Nelson's inspired leadership and concern for all who served under him. "No Captain can do very wrong," he had written a few days earlier, "if he places his ship alongside that of an Enemy."

OPPOSITE: The *Victory* in Portsmouth today, restored to her Trafalgar condition and flying the immortal signal "England Expects that Every Man will do his duty."

ABOVE: A seaman, by Rowlandson.

LEFT: The opening stage of the Battle of Trafalgar, 21 October 1805. The French and Spanish fleets, straggled in line close to the shore as they run for Cadiz, have opened fire. On the far right Collingwood's column has just reached the enemy line, while in the centre Nelson's column, with *Victory* at its head, has yet to engage.

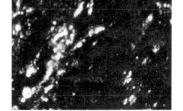

The 2,162-ton *Victory* was Nelson's flagship at Trafalgar. Designed by Sir Thomas Slade, Senior Surveyor to the Royal Navy, she had been launched at Chatham in 1765 as a first-rate ship of the line. From figurehead to taffrail she measured 226 feet, and her extreme beam was 52 feet. Between 1800 and 1802 she underwent a major refit before becoming, in 1803, Nelson's flagship. At that time Nelson was commander of the fleet that was blockading Villeneuve in Toulon. The French escaped in March 1805, and Nelson spent six months in pursuit, crossing to the West Indies and back again. At length Villeneuve was cornered off Trafalgar, and the die was cast.

As Nelson's line bore down on the Combined Fleet, *Victory*'s band struck up "Rule Britannia" and "Britons Strike Home." At this point the admiral decided "to amuse the fleet" by making the signal "England confides that every man will do his duty." The signal lieutenant responsible for hoisting aloft the combination of flags suggested "expects" for "confides," because the first word was in the signal book while "confides" would have to be spelt out letter by letter. Nelson agreed, and the famous signal was sent. It was followed immediately by another, conveyed by the simple number 16: "Close upon the enemy and begin action."

OPPOSITE: Horatio Lord Nelson (1758-1805). He is shown wearing the star of a Knight of the Bath and, around his neck, a medal awarded after the Battle of St Vincent in 1797. He lost his arm in the same year while attacking Tenerife.

BELOW: An 1807 painting of five ships on which Nelson served. From right to left they are the *Victory*, the *Captain*, the *Elephant*, the *Vanguard*, and the *Agamemnon*.

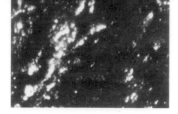

HMS Victory

54
—

A detail from William Turner's dramatic painting of the *Victory* at Trafalgar.

The fleets were now a mile apart, moving painfully slowly in the light north-northwest wind. Parallel with Nelson's line, to the south and slightly ahead of it, was the second British column under Vice-Admiral Cuthbert Collingwood in the *Royal Sovereign*. Collingwood was first to engage. Unable to bring his broadsides to bear during his approach, he endured strong enemy fire for the final thousand yards, until he reached Villeneuve's line. The *Royal Sovereign* passed close under the stern of the Spanish flagship *Santa Ana* and discharged her full port broadside into her adversary's unprotected stern. It smashed along the length of the *Santa Ana's* crowded decks, causing dreadful carnage. Then, in a confusion of rigging and spars, both ships crashed together to become enveloped in their own gunsmoke.

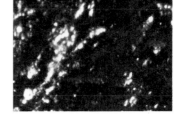

Ammunition of Nelson's day. Top centre and centre left, ball shot. Top right, canister shot. Left and right, chain shot. Bottom left and centre, bar shot. The extending shot at the bottom of the picture was used to cut down rigging.

A few minutes later *Victory* reached the line, loosing a murderous broadside into the stern of Villeneuve's flagship *Bucentaure* before ramming and engaging the French *Redoutable*. Close behind her three other British ships — *Temeraire*, *Neptune* and *Leviathan* — followed *Victory* through the gap. The "pell-mell battle" with Napoleon's main fleet, which Nelson had sought for so many years, had begun.

Victory and *Redoutable*, inextricably entangled, drifted down on the *Temeraire*, and then the three ships collided with the French *Fougaux*, so that all four became locked together side by side. *Victory's* port-side guns had to be loaded with reduced powder charges to prevent the shot from passing through *Redoutable* and into the *Temeraire*, while her starboard broadside continued to engage the four-decker Spanish *Santissima Trinidad* and the French flagship *Bucentaure*. The 74-gun *Redoutable*, with a 100-gun British ship on either side of her, took a fearful pounding, but her crew resisted with incredible gallantry and her captain, Jean-Jacques Lucas, refused to strike until 500 of his 600-strong company had been killed. *Redoutable's* achievements more than matched her name: not only had she reduced the *Victory* to a near-wreck but, just before she surrendered, a sharp-shooter stationed in her rigging mortally wounded Lord Nelson as he strode *Victory's* deck, conspicious in his admiral's uniform and orders of chivalry.

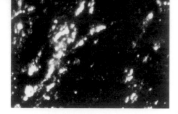

HMS Victory

The dying Admiral was carried to the cockpit on the orlop deck, where the wounded were tended — a place later described by the ship's chaplain as "like a butcher's shambles." There he lay until, at 4.30 in the afternoon, the final victory was reported to him. He died shortly afterwards. Eighteen enemy ships had surrendered, and one was burning out of control. Four others were captured some days later. *Victory* herself was severely damaged, with 57 of her crew killed and 103 wounded.

Trafalgar was the greatest, and almost the last, fleet action to be fought by sailing ships, and it represented the destructive high point of the age of fighting sail. Although Nelson's ships were superior in every respect to those of the previous three centuries, the *Victory* and her sisters were products of exactly the same technologies that had created the *Mary Rose* and the *Wasa*. True, they were bigger, and had a more refined sail plan. But their real advantages lay not so much in naval hardware as in the quality and skill of their men, the experience and leadership of their officers, and the massive (though in many ways corrupt) administrative system which backed them up.

The years spent at sea blockading Napoleon's fleets in their ports had bred hardy and disciplined crews who performed their duties with confidence and skill. Theirs was not a comfortable life, and it was sometimes one of extreme brutality, but the cat-o'-nine-tails could not of itself instill the efficient teamwork Nelson demanded, and it was little used on his ships. Pride, practice and competition were the watchwords, always spiced by the knowledge that a successful ship might win prize money which would be shared (though by no means equally) by all.

Something of the stern, heroic, yet surprisingly human, world of Nelson's navy survives in the fabric of the *Victory* herself, now magnificently preserved, and restored to her Trafalgar appearance, at Portsmouth. After the battle she was towed to Gibraltar for temporary repairs, and then sailed for Portsmouth bearing Nelson's body, pickled in a keg of brandy. She continued to see active service until 1812, and was extensively rebuilt between 1813 and 1816. From 1824 to the present day, except for the period between 1869 and 1889, she has been the flagship of the Portsmouth Command.

Until 1922 *Victory* remained afloat in Portsmouth harbor, though by then her timbers were dangerously decayed. In that year, however, she was placed in dry dock, and with the approval and co-operation of the Admiralty a public appeal was launched by the Society for Nautical Research to restore the ship as a national monument. The restoration was completed in 1928, and *Victory* (with *Mary Rose* and *Warrior* as worthy neighbors) is now Portsmouth's greatest attraction.

Visitors to the *Victory* enter, quite literally, Nelson's world. She sits proudly in the dock, her hull painted in the color scheme prescribed by Nelson for his fleet — bands of yellow on the line of the gun decks with stripes of black between. The outside of the port lids are also black, so that when closed they

News of the victory reaches England: headlines in the London *Times* of 7 November 1805.

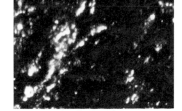

give a checkered effect. Her waterline is level with the dock edge to give an impression of how she looked when afloat. The lower hull is coppered with 3,923 pieces, each four feet by one foot, to protect her timbers from the ravages of teredo worm. This practice was introduced in 1780 to increase the endurance of ships on blockade.

Nelson placed emphasis on developing his crews' skill in handing the guns in concert with the ship, and encouraged them to practise using live ammunition. A treatise written in 1777 noted: "...it is necessary to let them smell powder, as it is termed. And a little ammunition spent in exercise if allowed, may be the means to save a great deal expended to little purpose in action..." The author went on to recommend dropping an empty cask over the side for target practise. If it was sunk the crews would be rewarded with an extra ration of grog; if they missed, they would have to hoist out the ship's boat and recover it. It was this emphasis on practise and competition that enabled Nelson's crews to serve their guns quickly and efficiently in the heat and confusion of battle, and to work the ships so that those guns could be used to the best possible effect.

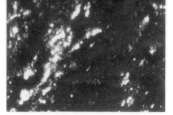

The figurehead dates from the refit of 1801–03, when *Victory* was being prepared for service as Nelson's flagship. It consists of an oval shield bearing the royal arms, with a crown above and the royal motto ''Dieu et mon droit'', below. Further decoration embellishes the beakhead, the entrance ports, and the great square stern.

Towering above the ship is her mainmast, 240 feet from keelson to truck, with a maximum girth of seven and a half feet. *Victory* is fully rigged, and from her halliards fly the flags which spell out Nelson's immortal signal.

The ship's interior is dominated by its three great gun decks. Visitors are immediately aware of the low headroom. Everything on the ship is subservient to the need to pack on board as many guns as possible, and three tiers of artillery can only be achieved at the expense of height. The lower, or main, gun deck is 186 feet long, and set only a few feet above the waterline. Ranged along its sides are 30 black cast-iron 32-pounders, each mounted on a yellow-painted truck carriage. Above it, the middle gun deck carries 28 24-pounders, and the upper gun deck 30 12-pounders. Fourteen more 12-pounders are mounted on the quarter-deck and forecastle. Also on the forecastle were two 68-pounder carronades — squat, close-range guns nicknamed ''smashers'' because of their destructive power.

Crews lived, ate, and slept between their guns. A 32-pounder required a team of fourteen to operate it and, since both broadsides would rarely be in action at the same time, the team was also responsible for the gun on the opposite side. Stowed beside each gun was its operating equipment — rammer, sponge, worm, and ready-use shot. Mess tables and benches were rigged between the guns, and here the crews messed; at night they slung their hammocks from the deck-beams above.

BELOW LEFT: An early nineteenth-century etching of seamen in their mess. Note the securely lashed cannon, the slung hammocks, and the gunnery implements and cutlasses hung ready for use.

BELOW RIGHT: Ship's purser: a sketch by Thomas Rowlandson, 1799.

The *Victory's* lower gun deck, with mess tables down and hammocks stowed. Rammers and ladles for the truck-mounted 32-pounders hang on the deck beams.

Two cold meals and one hot meal were provided each day. Food was basic: the hot meal was usually "duff," a kind of steamed flour pudding; the cold staple was ship's biscuit which, according to one who had to eat it, made the throat "cold in eating it, owing to the maggots . . ." The same writer describes the water, which might be stored for months on end in wooden casks, as "the colour of the bark of pear trees, with plenty of maggots and weevils in it." No wonder the twice-daily issue of rum was popular.

Along the center line of the lower two decks, apart from the masts, are the capstans, atop which the ship's fiddler would sit and play a tune as the men heaved on the capstan bars. Forward on the middle deck is the galley, lined with brick to make it fireproof. This is the only part of the ship where seamen were allowed to smoke.

At the after end of the main deck is the officers' wardroom and quarters; their private cubicles and furniture were capable of being instantly dismantled for stowage in the hold when the ship was cleared for action. Nelson's own quarters on the deck above also contained, discreetly hidden below chintz covers, their complement of 24-pounders, ready to become part of the broadside battery when need arose.

In the cockpit on the orlop deck, where Nelson died, is a shrine to his memory, and each Trafalgar Day wreaths are laid here. That this ceremony still takes place after nearly two centuries would surely have surprised the old admiral, whose genuine humility was an aspect of his greatness. But he would be deeply gratified to observe the sense of history and tradition of the young ratings who serve as guides aboard the *Victory*. As they show visitors around the ship and tell of her inspiring past they clearly demonstrate that the "Nelson touch" is still very much alive in Britain's modern navy.

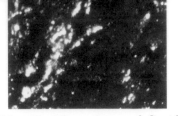

THE GOLDEN AGE OF SAIL

Some time before the dawn of recorded history, the world's more advanced civilizations developed wooden vessels capable of venturing out onto the open sea. The earliest were probably large dugout canoes. To keep the rough seas from pouring in, the sides of the dugouts were extended upwards by the addition of one or more horizontal planks. From this simple beginning the fully planked hull evolved.

The planks that extended the sides of the dugout had been fastened edge to edge, and early shipbuilders continued this system. Planks were sewn together, pegged together, or, where metal was available, stapled together. The Viking ships of Norway and Denmark, with their overlapped "clinker-built" sides, were probably the finest development of this system. One thousand years ago the Norsemen used such craft to cross the stormy North Atlantic to Greenland and Newfoundland.

By the 1300s a new technique that would revolutionize wooden ship-building was being adopted in Europe. Some now-forgotten shipwright discovered that by first erecting a complete skeleton of ribs and then attaching the planks directly to these, rather than to each other, a far stronger hull could be built.

These early ships carried a basic square rig that was poorly suited to long voyages where some of the sailing would have to be done into the prevailing winds. In the early 1400s ships began to be rigged with a combination of square and "fore and aft" sails. These were able to sail much closer than previous ships to the direction from which the wind was coming. Such innovations made possible the exploration of vast new worlds and their subsequent opening up to colonization and trade. At first this trade was controlled by royal monopolies; later it was handled by chartered companies such as the Dutch East India Company, owners of the famous *Batavia*, which came to grief in 1629.

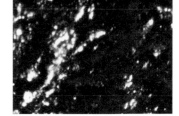

The Industrial Revolution, which had its beginnings in the 1700s, had profound implications for the sailing ship. As Europe's new manufacturing industries began to consume vast quantities of raw materials from around the globe, and went in search of ever wider export markets for their finished products, the demand for sailing vessels grew dramatically. Eventually, world trade became too complex to be controlled by a few chartered companies, and by the mid-1800s the last of these, the British East India Company, had passed out of existence.

Open international competition brought further advances in sailing ship design, the most spectacular being the development of the clipper ship. At the same time, builders of sailing ships were beginning to take advantage of the new technology of the industrial era. By the 1860s most deepwater sailing ships launched in the British Isles were either of composite construction, planked over iron ribs — or fully framed and plated with iron. By the 1880s good quality steel was being produced cheaply enough to allow most ships to be iron-plated.

The slow development of fuel-efficient marine steam engines meant that, in some long-distance trades, sailing ships remained viable until the early years of this century. By that time giant four- and five-masted vessels were being built that bore only a very basic resemblance to the small wooden sailing ships of a century earlier.

The deepwater sailing ship vanished from the world's trade routes within living memory. Many still wonder at the beauty of these ships, and at the skill and endurance it took to sail them. Historian Samuel Eliot Morison called such wooden clipper ships as *Flying Cloud* America's equivalent of the cathedrals of Europe. John Masefield, a poet laureate of England who went to sea in his youth, mourned: "They mark our passage as a race of men. Earth will not see such ships as these again."

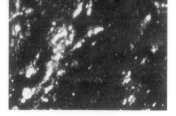

The V.O.C. flag at the bow of a
Dutch East Indiaman.

BATAVIA:

THE ILL-FATED EAST INDIAMAN

The Dutch colonial empire had its beginnings in the 1590s. By this time the Netherlands had freed itself from Spanish domination, and was enjoying great prosperity as the new trading center of northern Europe. Some of the wealth it had acquired was reinvested in trading expeditions to the East Indies. Portugal, which had opened these regions to trade less than a century earlier, had declined as a maritime power. Although England and France made attempts to compete with the Dutch, they could not match the financial resources of the cities of the Low Countries. There was a Dutch expedition to the Gold Coast of Africa in 1594, and the following year four ships flying the Dutch flag were in the East Indies trading for pepper. By 1598 the number of Dutch ships in the East had grown to twenty-two.

By 1602 each of the major cities of the Netherlands — Amsterdam, Rotterdam, Middelburg, Delft, Hoorn, and Enkhuizen — had sent out trading expeditions. In that year these cities combined their efforts and formed the Verenigde Oost-Indische Compagnie, or Dutch East India Company, often referred to simply by its initials as the "V.O.C." The new company was to have a monopoly on Dutch trade east of the Cape of Good Hope and west of the Straits of Magellan. It would also have the resources to send out fleets

A view, from the middle of the seventeenth century, of the Dutch colonial town of Batavia. Note the fortification of the old "Castle Batavia".

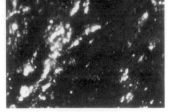

of large, well-armed vessels — to counter any Spanish or Portuguese efforts in the East, to gain the co-operation of local rulers, and to fight off pirates along the route.

In 1619 the Dutch founded a trading station near the west end of Java which they named Batavia, from the Latin designation for the Netherlands. Batavia, which is today the Indonesian city of Djakarta, soon became an important destination for the outward-bound fleets of the V.O.C.

In 1611 a Dutch commander named Hendrik Brouwer had discovered that by sailing due east (instead of north-east) from the Cape of Good Hope to the approximate longitude of Java, and then turning north, he could make the passage more quickly. The prevailing westerly winds in the low latitudes of the southern Indian Ocean drove his ship eastwards until it encountered winds from the south that carried it north to the Spice Islands. Five years later another Dutch commander, Dirk Hartog, sighted the west coast of Australia not far east of Brouwer's turning point.

Hartog's new land appeared to be worthless. There was no sign of a civilized population with which to trade, and the terrain was dry and barren. As well, the rugged coastline presented a serious threat to any navigator who miscalculated his eastward progress and failed to turn north in time. Unfortunately, accurate determination of longitude would not become possible until well into the following century, when the British developed the chronometer.

One extremely lucky Dutch commander who sailed too far east was Frederick Houtman. In July 1619 he encountered a hazard even more insidious than the cliffs of the mainland. Thirty-five miles west of the continent he sighted a group of small, low-lying islands surrounded by reefs, on which he only narrowly avoided being wrecked. The Dutch named them "Houtman's Abrolhos," borrowing the second word from the Portuguese who had used it to designate similar hazards to navigation elsewhere: "Abri vossos olhos!" — "Lookout!" (literally, "Open your eyes"). The most tragic victim of Houtman's Abrolhos was to be the V.O.C. flagship *Batavia*.

BELOW RIGHT: This shot along the deck of a replica of the *Batavia* gives a dramatic idea of how it must have felt to sail in her.

BELOW LEFT: Silverware which may have once graced the captain's table on the *Batavia,* or which formed part of the cargo.

The Batavia *would have been a typical East Indiaman of the period, in Dutch
terminology a retourschip. In 1624 the V.O.C. had set a maximum length for these
vessels of 160 feet. The corresponding breadth of hull would have been around 35
feet, and the depth of hold around fourteen feet. The East Indiamen bore a general
resemblance to warships of the same period. They were three-masted vessels with
square sterns, raised poops aft, and rows of gunports on either side. Their armament
was lighter than that of a warship, but they were quite able to defend themselves
against pirates and privateers, and to serve as the V.O.C.'s navy in the East.
The added space at the stern provided comfortable quarters for officers of the ship,
officials of the company, and any important people who were traveling first class.
Two or three continuous decks running the length of the ship would have provided
quarters for other passengers and crew. Below the lowest of these decks there would
have been an ample hold for stowing cargo.*

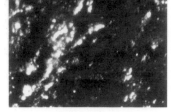

ABOVE RIGHT: In the foreground, a model of a Dutch East Indiaman of the time; and in the background, the restored timber and reconstructed hull of the *Batavia* itself, held in the Western Australian Maritime Museum in Fremantle.

BELOW: Silver coins salvaged from the wreck of the *Batavia*.

On her last voyage, in 1629, the *Batavia* had on board a total of 316 people, including a detachment of soldiers for the garrison at Batavia, and families on their way to settle in the new colony. In her strongroom she carried twelve chests of coins and jewels. One "Great Cameo," possibly designed by the painter Rubens, was intended for sale to Emperor Jehangir of India. Among other items in the hold were the cut and dressed stones for a handsome new gate to Batavia Castle.

The *Batavia* was flagship of a small fleet of vessels. On board was the commander of that fleet, Francis Pelsaert, one of the company's merchants. Captain of the *Batavia*, taking his orders from Pelsaert, was Ariaen Jacobsz. The supercargo, responsible for looking after the goods and passengers on board, was Jeronimus Cornelisz, a former druggist from Haarlem. As events were to prove, the appointments of both Jacobsz and Cornelisz to such import- ant positions were disastrous errors on the part of the V.O.C.

Pelsaert was the brother-in-law of Hendrik Brouwer, now an important offic- ial of the company. He and Jacobsz had quarrelled the last time they were associated. Jacobsz undoubtedly resented taking his orders from Pelsaert, whom he had previously known in lesser positions, and who had probably received this latest promotion largely through the influence of a relative. Jacobsz suffered from a number of serious character flaws, one of which was a propensity for heavy drinking. After a drinking bout on board another ship

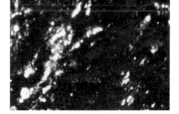

in Cape Town, Jacobsz had acted "very beastly with words as well as deeds;" he was severely reprimanded by Pelsaert who threatened to remove him from the command of the *Batavia*.

At some point Captain Jacobsz began to discuss the idea of mutiny with sympathetic members of the crew. According to the plan that was hatched, anyone on board who did not join them would be murdered or marooned. The *Batavia* would be sailed to a port that was not controlled by the Dutch, and all the mutineers would live as rich men from the treasure on board. The ship could also be used in a campaign of piracy against other Dutch East Indiamen. It was apparently decided that the plan would go into effect when the ship neared the coast of Australia.

Another of Jacobsz' weaknesses was lust. He had developed a compelling passion for Lucretia van der Mylen, a young woman passenger, who was to join her husband in Java. Having failed to seduce Lucretia, the captain turned his attentions to her maid, Zwaantie, who proved to be quite receptive. At least one crew member observed the couple, in flagrante delicto, in one of the ship's quarter-galleries.

Jacobsz continued to resent his rejection by Lucretia. He also hoped to provoke Pelsaert into an unpopular act of punishment that could be used to trigger the mutiny. One dark night, on Jacobsz' orders, Lucretia was attacked on deck by several disguised men; she was stripped naked, smeared with excrement and pitch, and dragged about by her legs. The victim recognized some of her attackers and, as Jacobsz expected, Pelsaert decided to deal with them severely when the ship made its first landfall. In the Netherlands at that time the punishment for "sexual offenses" was death.

ABOVE: A variety of items from *Batavia* wreck.

LEFT: Majolica pottery from the early seventeenth century, salvaged from the sea bed where it had sunk with the vessel.

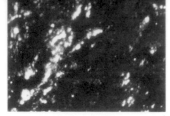

Batavia

This underwater photograph shows the stern timbers of the ill-fated *Batavia*, resting on Morning Reef in the Abrolhos.

Contact with the other ships of the fleet had been lost east of Cape Town, probably as part of Jacobsz' plan. On the night of 4 June Pelsaert was in his cabin sick. The weather was fine and there was a bright moon shining. Jacobsz later claimed that he saw surf in the distance but was told by the helmsman that it was only moonlight on the water. Soon afterwards the *Batavia* crashed into the reef surrounding Houtman's Abrolhos.

An attempt was made to lighten the vessel by throwing cannons overboard, but she had gone quite solidly aground too near high tide. The wind arose, moving the ship against the rocks in a way that threatened to grind open the hull. To ease this motion the mainmast was cut away, but the rigging remained attached to the ship and the floating spars threatened to further damage the planking. There was little discipline. Terror-stricken passengers cried out in fright at each new indication that the vessel might be breaking up, while some of the seamen broke into the wine and were soon adding to the chaos with drunken carousing.

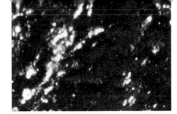

Batavia

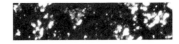

ABOVE: This view of Morning Reef clearly shows the heavy surf line, against which the *Batavia* met her doom.

ABOVE LEFT: The anchor of the unlucky ship on the ocean floor.

In two of the ship's boats, a shallop and a skiff, 180 people, along with twenty barrels of bread and some water, were ferried to two small barren islands. Larger islands could be seen to the north and Pelsaert set off in one of the boats to see if any fresh water could be found there. He located ample fresh water among the rocks, but decided it was too contaminated by sea water to be usable.

Pelsaert now decided to take the search for water to the mainland of Australia. The larger boat was given a deck to make it more seaworthy, and a crew was assembled. Captain Jacobsz, accompanied by his mistress, went along as navigator. The mainland was found easily enough, but it took days to find a safe place to go ashore, and even longer to find water. In the process, Pelsaert became the first European to land on Western Australia and record details of the terrain and its inhabitants.

As the days passed, the small boat and its contingent moved steadily closer to the Dutch settlements on Java. Pelsaert finally decided not to return to the Abrolhos, but instead to sail the boat to Batavia and find a ship there with which to rescue the rest of his people. He arrived there with 45 survivors on 3 July 1629.

Back on the islands events had taken a bloody turn. The seventy or so men still on the ship had managed to get ashore on floating wreckage. The last to leave the *Batavia* was the supercargo Jeronimus Cornelisz. In the absence of Pelsaert and the captain he was now the senior officer. He had also been one of the leaders of the planned mutiny.

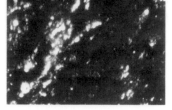

Batavia

7 0

An illustration from a 1648 publication, *Unlucky Voyage of the Ship Batavia,* depicts the cruel violence among the mutineers.

Cornelisz learned that, in a drunken moment, a crew member had revealed the existence of the plot. He assembled the conspirators and presented a new plan. Although the *Batavia* could not be salvaged, Cornelisz and his men could surprise and capture the ship that came to rescue them and still escape with the treasure. The passengers, meanwhile, were no longer simply a hindrance; with what they now knew they could have the conspirators tortured and hanged. Cornelisz used his authority as senior officer to distribute people, in smaller groups, throughout the islands. Thus divided up, they were systematically murdered. A group of more than 40 soldiers had been sent without weapons to one of the larger islands to the north, supposedly to look for water. Finding drinkable water, they lighted three fires as the agreed-upon signal. There was no response from the smaller island, where a massacre was now being carried out.

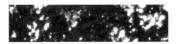

Batavia

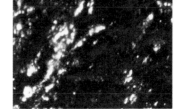

7 1
—

One seaman managed to escape on a raft, and informed the soldiers of what was happening. Under the leadership of a sergeant, Wiebe Hays, they built a small fort and armed themselves with stones and wooden staves. When Cornelisz launched an attack with his well-armed men he was repulsed with casualties. He then pretended to negotiate with Hays, while slipping the offer of a bribe to some of Hays' men, who told their leader of the offer. The next time Cornelisz set foot on the island he was attacked; his two lieutenants were killed and he himself was captured. The remaining mutineers were launching another attack on Wiebe Hays and his men when the rescue ship appeared. Hays managed to reach the ship and tell Pelsaert what had happened in his absence, and the mutineers were captured without a struggle.

Very few people had been lost coming ashore from the wreck, but 125 had been murdered on the islands by Cornelisz and his men. The only ones spared

This picture shows the punishments and executions meted out to the mutineers of the *Batavia*. Above we see the gibbets on the Abrolhos, and the condemned men having their hands severed. Below, torture and death are administered in Batavia.

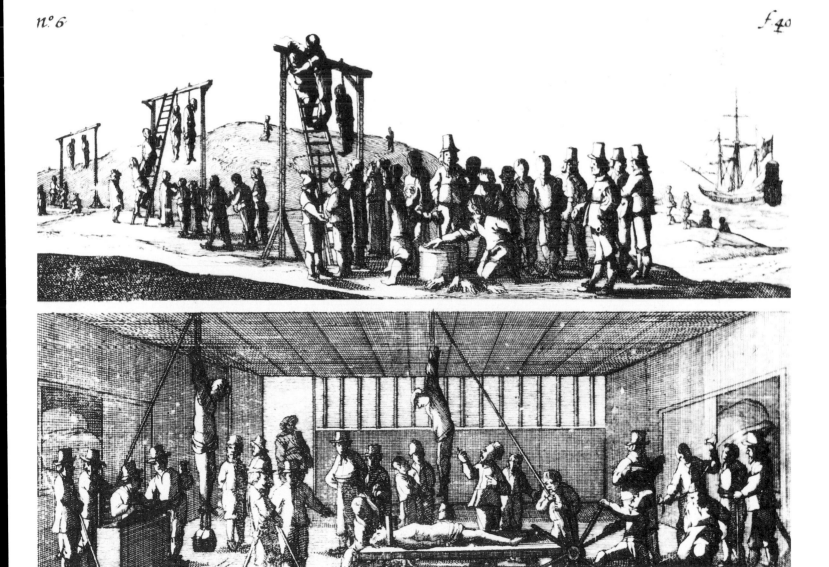

n.° 6

f. 40

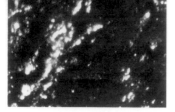

were a few women who were forced to serve as concubines, and a minister. Among the surviving women was Lucretia van der Mylen, whom Cornelisz had chosen for his own bed. She had resisted his advances for twelve days, but finally gave in when threatened with imminent death.

More than 30 men had been involved in the mutiny. Rather than try to transport this many to Batavia, Pelsaert decided to deal with the leaders at the scene of their crimes. Torture was the accepted means of determining guilt at this time, and it was used to extract detailed confessions, which are still in existence. Eight men were sentenced to hang, among them Cornelisz who, before being executed, had both hands chopped off at the wrist. Most of the others had one hand cut off. Before leaving the islands, Pelsaert succeeded in salvaging ten of the twelve chests of treasure the *Batavia* had been carrying.

The bloody events surrounding the wreck of the *Batavia* were a popular subject for authors for years afterwards. They had not been forgotten in 1840 when the HMS *Beagle*, on one of its voyages of research, visited the islands off the west coast of Australia. A surveyor on board, Lieutenant Crawford Pascoe, found wooden wreckage on a beach and attributed it to the ill-fated Dutch East Indiaman. He was actually 60 miles south of the site of the wreck. For the next century historians accepted Pascoe's placement of the ship's last resting place.

Then an Australian author, Henrietta Drake-Brockman, decided to use the story of the *Batavia* as the basis for a novel. After reading a copy of Pelsaert's journal, obtained from the Dutch archives in 1948, she concluded that the wreck must actually lie in the northern Abrolhos. In 1960 divers began a

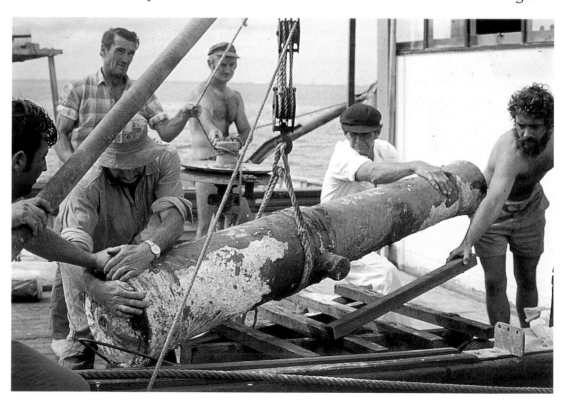

The salvage crew raises cannon from the wreck.

systematic search for the *Batavia* off the smaller islands of that group. An anchor, found by a lobster fisherman in June 1963, finally led them to the remains of the ship, which was lying in eighteen feet of water.

The *Batavia* has proved to be the richest archaeological find in the waters of Western Australia. In addition to cannon, coins, jewelry, navigational instruments, and silver utensils, a large portion of the ship's stern, with much of its lower transom planking intact, was eventually salvaged. The finished stones which the ship was carrying for a gateway arch in the city of Batavia can now be seen, fully assembled, in the Western Australian Museum at Fremantle.

A diver investigates *Batavia*'s sunken cannon.

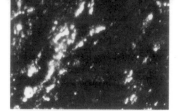

Cutty Sark

The *Cutty Sark* at Greenwich. The white-painted figurehead can be seen under the bowsprit.

CUTTY SARK:

IN HONOUR OF A DANCING WITCH

For anyone fascinated by things maritime, a highlight of a visit to London has to be the launch trip down the Thames, from the center of the city to Greenwich. This riverside Georgian suburb is the home of the grand Royal Naval Hospital, designed by Britain's leading architects of the eighteenth century, including Sir Christopher Wren. It is also the home of Britain's National Maritime Museum, the original Greenwich Astronomical Observatory, and the world's only restored clipper chip, *Cutty Sark*.

Resting in a stone drydock, *Cutty Sark* greets the visitor just beyond the gates to the boat landing. Its towering masts are rigged as though ready for sea, and its long jib boom points toward the muddy waters of the Thames. Stone steps allow the visitor to descend into the drydock and stand in front of the knife-like stem. The sight of that bow conveys, far better than words, exactly what made some sailing vessels "clipper ships".

By repealing its Navigation Acts in 1848, Great Britain opened the tea trade between Chinese and British ports to American clippers. In 1850 the American *Oriental* arrived in London after a record passage of 97 days. The Scottish firm of Alexander Hall & Co., located in Aberdeen, had been building smaller fine-lined sailing vessels since their schooner *Scottish Maid* of 1839. In 1850 they received the order for the first British clipper ship, *Stornoway*, a vessel of 506 tons.

Larger clippers were needed to compete with the American vessels. When the *Oriental* returned to London in 1851 she was drydocked and her lines were recorded by Admiralty surveyor Bernard Waymouth, who would later design the British clipper ships *Leander* and *Thermopylae* of the 1860s. In 1852 Alexander Hall & Co. launched the 1,250-ton *Cairngorm*, a vessel capable of matching the performance of the American clippers.

Three years later the Aberdeen shipyard took on a nineteen-year-old apprentice named Hercules Linton. His six-year term as an apprentice shipwright would have lasted until the end of 1860. The son of a marine surveyor for Lloyd's, Linton initially went into his father's profession, providing information on the seaworthiness of new vessels for the use of prospective insurers. By 1866 he was also designing ships, and two years later he established his own shipyard at Dumbarton, Scotland, in partnership with 23-year-old William Dundas Scott. Over the next two years they built nine vessels, all designed by Linton. The first six were steamers. The seventh was the iron sailing ship *Invereshie*, and the eighth the composite clipper ship *Cutty Sark*.

The *Cutty Sark* was built for John and Robert Willis of London, who had inherited the shipowning business from their father, John Willis Sr., in 1862. The brothers had acquired several second-hand sailing ships, but *Cutty Sark*

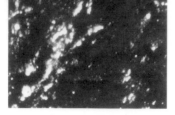

Cutty Sark

7 6

ABOVE: Guests aboard the *Cutty Sark* in her early days.

ABOVE RIGHT: A view of the starboard side of the hull.

was the first vessel built for them. One of their purchases had been the former Indian Marine paddle-steamer *Punjaub*. They converted her to a sailing vessel and renamed her the *Tweed*. She is said to have proved so satisfactory that some of her hull lines were incorporated into the design of the *Cutty Sark*.

John Willis, a well-known figure on the London maritime scene, was clearly the senior member of the partnership. He was generally referred to either as "Jock Willis" or "Old White Hat". The latter nickname derived from the immaculate white top hat he wore on all occasions. When one of his ships was sailing from London it was customary for the apprentices to line the rail and salute him by raising their caps and calling out "Good-bye Sir," to which Willis would respond by raising his white top hat and calling out "Good-bye, my lads." The fine carved decoration on the counter of the *Cutty Sark* still displays, in gilded lettering, the play on words, "Where there's a Willis a Way."

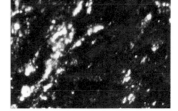

The Willis family came from the border country between England and Scotland, and most of their ships carried names that referred to places around the valley of the Tweed River. In choosing a name for their Scottish-built tea clipper they borrowed from one of the poems of Robert Burns. Tam O'Shanter's exclamation "Weel doon cutty sark!" must have appealed to Jock Willis, who had hopes of seeing his clipper arrive home with the first tea of the season and a new record for the passage.

Tam O'Shanter, who was spying secretly on a gathering of witches, was exclaiming over the dancing of the young witch, Nannie, who was clad only in a short chemise, or "cutty sark." After giving himself away by his enthusiasm, Tam had to ride hard to escape across the Brig o'Doon: witches were unable to follow across flowing water. In her pursuit, Nannie had come close enough to pull off the tail of Tam's horse. The figurehead of the *Cutty Sark*, which depicts Nannie in her chemise, should, to be complete, have the horse's tail clasped in its outstretched left hand.

Hercules Linton's original sketch of Nannie the witch as he imagined her for the figurehead, clad only in a "cutty sark" and grasping the escaping horse's tail in her hand.

The agreed price for building the *Cutty Sark* was only £16,150, or £17 per ton. The money was to be paid in eight instalments which would come due at specific points during the construction. The keel was laid in February 1869, and the finished vessel was due to be delivered on or before 30 July of the same year. The *Cutty Sark* was still on the ways when the shipbuilding firm of Scott & Linton failed financially in September 1869. The Scott & Linton creditors turned over completion of the ship to William Denny & Brothers of Dumbarton.

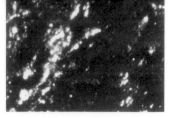

"CUTTY SARK."

The *Cutty Sark* depicted in the
splendor of full sail.

Cutty Sark

79

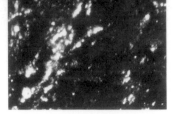

ABOVE: The ship's galley.

ABOVE RIGHT: The elegant tracery of the *Cutty Sark*'s yards.

The *Cutty Sark* was launched on 22 November 1869. She was christened by the wife of Captain George Moodie, who had been chosen to command the ship and who had supervised her construction on behalf of the owners. The ship was moved to the Denny shipyard to have the masts put in, and then across the Clyde to Greenock, where the rigging was completed. In the Clyde estuary off Greenock the ship would have been "turned" on a range of two fixed points ashore to have the error in the magnetic compasses determined and adjusted. The *Cutty Sark* sailed from Greenock on 13 January 1870 for London, where she would load her first cargo in the East India Docks.

The *Cutty Sark* had been designed to take part in the annual race home with Chinese tea. Unfortunately, she was completed just as the heyday of that trade was passing for sailing ships. In 1869 the Suez Canal had been opened. Steamships, no longer handicapped by the long passage around Africa, could now carry the tea to Europe in a month less than the time taken by the fastest clippers. For a time, shippers of the highest quality teas continued to use sailing ships in the belief that their wood-planked hulls preserved the cargo better than the steamers' iron hulls.

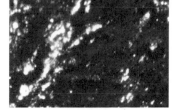

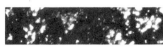

Cutty Sark

The *Cutty Sark* remained in the trade until 1877, making the usual single voyage out and back each year. Her voyage times were good, but did not set any new records. The ship Jock Willis particularly wanted to beat was the *Thermopylae*, a clipper one year older than the *Cutty Sark*, which had set a record for the passage to Australia by sailing from London to Melbourne in just 60 days.

In 1872 the conditions were ideal for a race home from China between the two vessels. Both loaded their tea in Shanghai, and both departed the river on 18 June. They sighted each other off Hong Kong, and did not completely lose contact again until 25 July. Beginning on 11 August, the *Cutty Sark* experienced a series of gales. At 6:30 on the morning of the 15th a wave struck the stern with such force that it tore off the ship's rudder.

Robert Willis, who was on board as a passenger, suggested putting into Cape Town for repairs. Captain Moodie decided instead to fabricate a jury rudder at sea and continue the voyage. A spare spar carried on deck was cut into three segments. These were fastened together to form the blade of the rudder, with one longer than the others to serve as the rudder post. In spite of continuing heavy seas, the makeshift rudder was manoevered under the stern and up into the trunk designed to house the rudder post.

This old photograph of men at the yards in high seas demonstrates the difficulty of seamanship in rough weather on the old clipper ships.

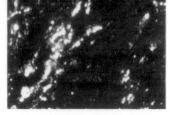

The new rudder was quite successful. The *Cutty Sark* was able to make the passage from the Cape of Good Hope to the English Channel in the very good time of 54 days. She had been delayed thirteen days by the mishap, but arrived only a week behind the *Thermopylae*. Fans of the *Cutty Sark* cite this as proof she was the faster vessel. Captain Moodie received much praise for his feat. This was his last voyage in command of the clipper ship. He now left the employment of Jock Willis to take over command of a steamship.

On three occasions in her long career, the Cutty Sark's *rudder was damaged. The first disaster occurred in August 1872 when she was racing the* Thermopylae *from China to London. A gale tore off the rudder and Captain Moodie decided to make a jury rudder at sea and continue the race, which the* Cutty Sark *finished only five days after her rival. That jury rudder is pictured here.*

The second accident occurred in a hurricane off Florida in September 1906, when the ship sank beside a pier, forcing the replacement of her rudder but causing little other damage.

The third occasion was in 1915, when her American-made rudder was lost at sea and Captain Souza brought her into port with a jury rudder.

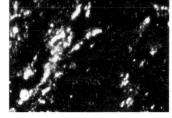

Cutty Sark

The stern of the *Cutty Sark*.

The next captain was F. W. Moore, a competent shipmaster who maintained the *Cutty Sark* like a fine yacht. Captain Moore had the ship only briefly, before taking a position ashore with the company. He was succeeded by Captain W. E. Tiptaft, who turned out to be something of a "driver". In 1874 he sailed the ship out to China by way of Sydney, Australia. Her performance on this passage was excellent: during one six-day period she logged 2,163 miles, and more than once she covered 370 miles in 24 hours. She was south of Melbourne just 64 days after leaving England.

When the China trade ceased to be profitable the *Cutty Sark* went into general trading, taking cargoes wherever she could find them. In 1880 she carried wool from Melbourne to New York. The following year she carried baled jute from the Philippines to New York, and loaded 26,816 cases of kerosene there for Samarang.

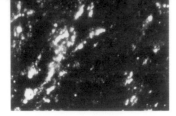

This period represents the low point in the vessel's career. Under two successive captains there were incidents involving brutality or the general mistreatment of seamen. In 1880, for example, the mate killed a black seaman by striking him with a capstan bar. The captain helped the mate escape and so avoid prosecution. Later, apparently depressed over what he had done, the captain committed suicide by jumping overboard at sea.

In 1883 the ship once again came into her own. That year Jock Willis sent her out to Australia to load wool for England. She remained in that trade for the next twelve years, commanded for the last ten by Captain Richard Woodget. For each of those ten years the *Cutty Sark* made the fastest homeward passage by a sailing vessel. Her fastest time from Sydney to the English Channel was 67 days; her slowest was only 90 days. She consistently beat her old rival, *Thermopylae*, until that vessel was sold to Canadian owners in 1890.

Because of its relatively light weight, wool filled up a ship's hold long before she was immersed to her maximum safe draft. To allow as much as possible to be carried, the wool was literally "screwed" into the hold with hand-operated presses. The *Cutty Sark* loaded her largest wool cargo, 5,304 bales, in 1895. It was the last one she would carry under the British flag. Steamers, and larger steel sailing vessels, were now taking over. Soon after she arrived in London, the *Cutty Sark* was sold by Jock Willis to Portuguese owners.

Officers and apprentices aboard the *Cutty Sark* in the last ten years of her service in the wool trade with Australia. Captain Richard Woodget is on the left.

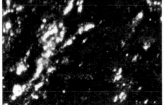

Cutty Sark

She sailed under the Portuguese flag for another 27 years, first under the name *Ferreira*, and after 1920 as the *Mario do Amparo*. In September 1906 she was caught in port at Pensacola, Florida, by a major hurricane, and sank beside a long pier that extended out into Pensacola Bay. Although the ship was assumed by the local papers to be a total loss, her hull, now almost 40 years old, turned out to need only minor repairs. Her rudder, however, had once more to be replaced.

In 1915 she lost her American-made rudder at sea. Captain Souza repeated Captain Moodie's feat of 1872 and brought the ship into port with a jury rudder. Shortly after this she was largely dismasted in a gale after a cargo of coal shifted to one side. A steamship towed her into Cape Town where, because suitable spars were not available, she was re-rigged as a barkentine.

The *Cutty Sark* was now the last of the legendary clipper ships still calling at British ports. Her visit to London in June 1919 attracted considerable interest from the press, and from sailing ship veterans and enthusiasts. In January 1922 she put into Falmouth on the south coast for repairs. She was seen there by Captain Wilfred Dowman, a sailing ship veteran, who decided to preserve her for future generations by buying her and using her as a floating maritime school, anchored near that port.

The romantic clipper, ocean bound.

When Captain Dowman died in 1936 his widow donated the ship, along with money for her upkeep, to the Thames Nautical Training College, located at Greenhithe below London. The school towed her to the Thames and moored her off Greenhithe next to their primary facility, the old wooden warship *Worcester*. In 1949, the school, which no longer used the *Cutty Sark* for training, offered her to the National Maritime Museum at Greenwich.

The museum did not feel it had the resources to take on preservation of a ship, but Frank Carr, the director of the museum, did not want to see the *Cutty Sark* scrapped. Under the auspices of a "Cutty Sark Preservation Society," he led a campaign to fund the restoration of the ship and the creation of a permanent berth for her at Greenwich. The London County Council gave its support to the project, and His Royal Highness, the Duke of Edinburgh, agreed to serve as patron. A stone drydock was built for the ship at Greenwich, and, through the research of naval architect and historian George Campbell, she was carefully restored to her original appearance. On 25 June 1957 *Cutty Sark* was officially opened to the public by Queen Elizabeth II.

Frank Carr went on to campaign for a British National Maritime Trust in order to save other important historic vessels. His efforts finally met with success in 1970, and some time later the *Cutty Sark* organization was merged with the National Maritime Trust. A few years ago, in recognition of the role played by the famous clipper in the creation of a maritime preservation movement in Great Britain, the National Maritime Trust was renamed the Cutty Sark Maritime Trust.

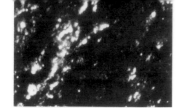

Preussen

A model of the *Preussen,* made by Carl Danielson of New York.

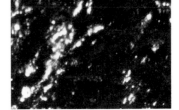

PREUSSEN:

THE "PRIDE OF PRUSSIA"

Sailing ship operation by the firm of F. Laeisz of Hamburg, Germany, spanned exactly a century. In 1839 the founder, Ferdinand B. Laeisz, had the 220-ton wooden brig *Carl* built in Lübeck, Germany, for trading with South America. When World War II broke out in the fall of 1939 the company still had two sailing ships in active service. Over that 100 years the sailing vessels operated by F. Laeisz evolved steadily. By the 1850s the company was operating 500-ton wooden barks, by the 1870s 1,000-ton iron full-rigged ships, and by the 1890s 2,800-ton four-masted barks. In 1902 it had the world's only five-masted full-rigged ship, *Preussen,* built. At 5,081 tons, she was the largest vessel ever built that was powered solely by the wind.

British shipbuilders had begun producing four-masted square-rigged vessels in the mid-1870s. By that decade, steamships were not only becoming competitive through the development of more efficient engines, they were becoming larger as well. Sailing ships would have to follow suit in order to survive. The use of iron had made the construction of larger ships feasible. Wooden hulls could only be built to a certain length before they lost their longitudinal strength. Iron hulls could be given effective longitudinal strengthening that took up little space.

In order to keep the rig of these larger vessels manageable, and economical to maintain and operate, an extra mast was added so that the individual sails could be kept virtually the same size. The sails were made relatively shallow by having five or six to a mast. This saved crew costs since it kept to a minimum the number of men needed out on a yard to furl a sail. The first three masts of a four-masted vessel were given identical dimensions. As the gear was interchangeable from mast to mast, it could be fabricated and replaced more economically.

In the late 1800s F. Laeisz came to specialize in the transport of nitrate from northern Chile around Cape Horn to European ports. Sodium nitrate, mined in the desert a short distance from the Pacific Ocean, found a ready market as a fertilizer for the worn-out farmlands of Europe. It could also be used in the manufacture of the explosive nitroglycerine.

The Hamburg company's leading competitor in the nitrate trade was the French firm of Anton Bordes et Fils, based in Bordeaux. In 1890 Anton Bordes took the unprecedented step of having a five-masted bark built in a British shipyard. Named the *France,* she measured 3,813 gross tons and could carry 6,200 tons of nitrate. The only previous five-masted sailing ships had been a handful of schooner-rigged vessels built for the American coastal trades, and one barkentine built for the Great Lakes. The *France* proved to be successful. In 1892 she made the passage from Dunkirk to Chile in the good

Preussen

The *Preussen*'s low lines gave her a
racy look under sail.

time of 74 days. In spite of this, Anton Bordes et Fils never owned another
five-master.

In fact, only one other five-masted bark was built without an engine. She
was the *Potosi*, launched in 1895 at the shipyard of J. C. Tecklenborg in
Geestemunde, Germany, to the order of F. Laeisz. The *Potosi* measured over
4,000 gross tons. On her maiden voyage she sailed from Germany to Chile in
73 days, taking only 66 days from the English Channel. The *Potosi* sailed for
the company until the outbreak of World War I. She was interned during the
war at Valparaiso, and after the war was awarded to France. In September
1925, while sailing under the Chilean flag, she caught fire and burned off the
coast of Argentina.

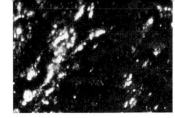

A view of the *Preussen* under sail from the port side.

The building of the giant *Preussen* in 1902 is difficult to understand in purely economical terms. F. Laeisz had not operated four-masted full-rigged ships. A number had been built in Great Britain, and many of these had had the yards removed from the fourth mast, making them into four-masted barks. This, however, had not significantly affected their performance, which clearly suggested that the added expense of having the last mast square-rigged was not really justified.

The *Preussen* had a hull 433 feet in length, 100 feet longer than the largest four-masted sailing vessel. Measuring all the way to the end of her bowsprit, she spanned a distance of 490 feet. She had a width of 54 feet, and her 46 sails had a total area of 60,000 square feet. The distance from the keel to the truck of her mainmast was 227 feet. Her lower yards were 100 feet in length, and each one weighed six and a half tons. Her rigging required 25 miles of wire, hemp, and Manila rope.

The five masts were named: foremast, mainmast, middlemast, Laeisz mast, and mizzenmast. The first four were identical. A crew of only 48 was carried to handle this giant rig. Many American clipper ships of the 1850s had had crews of 50 men.

Like the company's four-masted barks, she had a "three-island" deck layout: raised foredeck, raised midship deck, and raised poop. This allowed much of the rigging to be handled above the main deck which would be awash in heavy weather when the vessel was loaded. Catwalks connected the three decks. She was steered from the midship deck, under which the crew living quarters

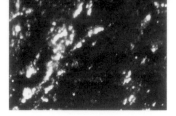

were located. Two steam boilers were carried in a forward deckhouse which could be used to power the anchor windlass, cargo winches, and – particularly unusual for a Cape Horn sailing vessel – the steering gear.

The *Preussen* was launched on 7 May 1902 at the yard of J. C. Tecklenborg in Geestemunde, Germany. She sailed for Chile on her maiden voyage on 31 July of that year. Her time for the passage was 69 days from Germany, and 65 from the English Channel. Except for a voyage around the world made in 1908, her entire career was spent in the trade with the west coast of South America.

There was obviously a great deal of nationalistic pride involved in the creation of the Preussen. *Her name meant "Prussia," and, like all F. Laeisz ships, she displayed the national flag of Germany in her color scheme. Her topsides were black, the area between loaded and empty waterlines was white, and her bottom was red – the same horizontal bands of color as the flag. Germans called her the "Pride of Prussia," and the "Queen of the Sea." Her birth came at a time when much of Germany's national pride centered around the sea. Germany's Navy was now a serious rival to Great Britain's, a German passenger liner had captured the coveted Blue Riband of the Atlantic, and the national flag now flew over a worldwide colonial empire.*

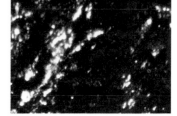

A model of the *Preussen*, giving
a clear picture of the sails and
rigging of this unique five-masted
ship.

Outward voyages were made with cargoes of fuels, coal or coke, or man-
ufactured goods. Loading in Europe was done with modern shore equipment:
shutes, conveyors, and dock cranes. In South America the cargo had to be discharged by more primitive means: using the ship's gear or the backs of long-
shoremen. The size of the *Preussen* was a disadvantage because there was
rarely enough outward cargo to fill the vessel, and on most passages she sailed
with some of her hold empty.

The Chilean ports were undeveloped open roadsteads, and the ships had to
anchor offshore, usually with moorings at both bow and stern. Even in good
weather majestic swells rolling in from some distant disturbance could set the
sailing ships rolling too violently for lighters to come alongside. When hurricane force storms, called "northers," struck, it was better for the ships to
weigh anchor and ride them out with plenty of sea room. Ships that did not
get clear of the anchorage stood a good chance of being driven ashore on a
rocky coastline.

The nitrate came on board in bags that were hoisted, usually one at a time,
from a lighter alongside by means of primitive hand-operated winches. Each
bag was lowered into the hold where a Chilean longshoreman took it on his
back, and skillfully tipped it into a precise location on the growing stack. The
F. Laeisz Company had built up an efficient operation on the Chilean coast,
eliminating the delays that other sailing ships were subject to as they waited
for cargo or available lighters. The stay in port at that end of the voyage could
usually be kept to about two weeks.

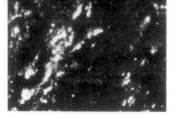

A newspaper photograph of the *Preussen* at the time of her visit to New York.

The nitrate ports of northern Chile, lying on a barren coastline with nothing but desert inland, had little to offer seamen. In the nineteenth century certain rituals, which continued to be observed as long as sailing ships called at the west coast ports, developed to celebrate the end of loading cargo and the final preparations for the homeward voyage. When the last bag of nitrate was hoisted out of the lighter alongside, the youngest seaman in the ship's crew, waving the flag of his country, rode aloft. Every man in the crew was issued a ration of rum or "schnapps." That night a wooden framework, displaying lanterns in the form of the constellation known as the "Southern Cross," was hoisted in the rigging. Bells of the other ships in the anchorage were rung one after another as a salute to the homeward-bound vessel.

On sailing day the captains of the other ships were rowed over for a visit. The apprentices or seamen in their boat crews assisted in weighing anchor, walking around the capstan on the forecastle head singing homeward-bound shanties. When the ship, with a few sails set, finally moved through the achorage towards the open sea, she was cheered by each of the vessels she passed.

The *Preussen* left the nitrate trade just once during her career. Early in 1908 she was chartered by the Standard Oil Company to carry a cargo from New York to Yokohama. She arrived at New York in ballast in April of that year and was towed to Pier 3, Bush Terminal, Brooklyn, to discharge. Once the ballast was out she was moved across the harbor to Constable Hook, Bayonne, New Jersey, the location of a large Standard Oil refinery and storage facility. As the ship was not fitted to carry liquids in bulk, the cargo had to be loaded in rectangular cans stowed with wooden separation. This "case oil" was mostly kerosine, the legendary "oil for the lamps of China" which was also shipped to Japan, Indochina, Burma, and India.

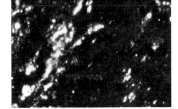

Preussen

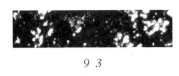

The visit of the giant sailing ship was well covered by the New York papers. Because it would be such a long voyage, Captain Boye Petersen had taken along his wife and young son. Two-year-old Heine Petersen, "the littlest sailor…on the biggest sailing ship," was particularly popular with the news photographers.

The *Preussen* sailed from New York at the end of May, heading south in the Atlantic and then turning east around the Cape of Good Hope. She rode the "roaring forties" across the southern Indian Ocean, and then headed north close to the west coast of Australia. Passing through the channels between Java and Timor, and Borneo and the Celebes, she arrived at Yokohama in mid-September. Leaving there the following month, she completed her circumnavigation of the globe by crossing the Pacific and taking a cargo of nitrate from Tocopilla, Chile, around Cape Horn to Hamburg.

New York Harbor in the first decade of the century.

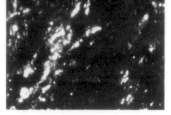

The *Preussen*, wrecked below the cliffs of Dover, where her remains lie to this day.

Captain Boye Petersen had commanded the *Preussen* since her maiden voyage. After completing this trip around the world he took a position ashore with the company turning over command of the giant sailing ship to Captain J. Hinrich Nissen, who had just spent five years as master of the *Potosi*. Under Nissen's command the *Preussen* completed two more voyages to Chile. She sailed on what would have been her fourteenth voyage on 31 October 1910.

Five days later disaster struck in the congested English Channel. The *Preussen* had passed the narrow point of the Channel at Dover, and was off Eastbourne, further to the west, when she collided with the British cross-channel steamer *Brighton,* bound from Newhaven to Dieppe in France. The steamer, underestimating the speed of the *Preussen,* tried to pass across her bow in clear violation of the nautical rules of the road. She was struck amidships by the sailing ship, sustaining considerable damage to her superstructure.

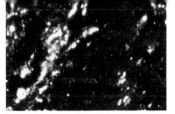

The *Preussen* was also damaged above the waterline. There were holes in her bow plating, her bowsprit was gone, and her foremast had partly collapsed. At this point the situation did not seem particularly serious. Captain Nissen arranged to have a tug tow the ship into Portsmouth, some distance to the west, for repairs.

The weather soon began to deteriorate. When strong winds developed from the west it was decided to come about and head east for Dover. Three tugs were now employed, two towing ahead and one alongside. The *Preussen* was only minutes from the safe shelter of the Dover breakwater when the gale force winds snapped one of the tow lines. The tugs could no longer manage the ship. Captain Nissen cast off the remaining tow line and began to set sail in an attempt to move away from the coast. The ship was almost clear when its keel struck a submerged rock. The *Preussen* was pivoted around by the wind and firmly grounded on a reef below Dover's famous white cliffs.

The *Preussen* was never refloated. Soon after she went ashore a severe crack developed in the hull. Much of the cargo was later salvaged and from time to time until 1925 parts of the ship were scrapped. The rest was abandoned. Wreckage could still be seen sticking out of the water in the late 1950s. As recently as the mid-1980s, when looking down from the cliffs on a calm day, one could still see the ship's submerged keel.

An official investigation of the loss of the ship cleared Captain Nissen and his officers of any responsibility, placing the blame squarely on the steamer *Brighton*. Nissen was subsequently given command of the four-masted bark *Peking*, which was nearing completion at Hamburg. He made his last voyage for F. Laeisz, as captain of that ship, in 1926. Retired from the nitrate trade in 1933, the *Peking* survives today as a floating museum in New York.

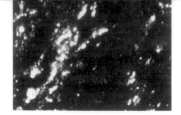

Sobraon

A dramatic painting of the *Sobraon* by J. Spurling.

SOBRAON:
THE LARGEST OF HER KIND

The world's last sailing passenger liners operated in the late 1800s between Great Britain and Australia. There were passenger steamships on this run by the early 1850s, and by 1869 they were able to take advantage of the shorter route by way of the Suez Canal. Yet, into the 1890s, many travellers chose instead to make the voyage in a sailing ship around the Cape of Good Hope. The continuing popularity of these ships was undoubtedly due, at least in part, to reasonable fares; but also important were the ships' comfortable accommodations, and the fact that they were well maintained and efficiently operated.

One of the most popular sailing ships on the route was the *Sobraon*, owned by Devitt & Moore of London. Like the *Cutty Sark*, she was a full-rigged ship with a composite hull, planked with teak over iron frames. In fact, she was the largest composite sailing ship ever built, having an overall hull length of 317 feet and a registered displacement of 2,131 tons.

Sobraon was built in 1866 at the yard of Alexander Hall & Co. in Aberdeen, Scotland — the same yard that had produced the first British clipper ships. Her first owners were Shaw, Lowther & Maxton of London who chartered the ship to Devitt & Moore for her first five voyages between that port and Sydney, Australia. After these voyages she was purchased by Devitt & Moore and shifted to the service between London and Melbourne, where she remained until the end of her seagoing career.

Sobraon was not an extreme clipper ship, but her hull lines were nonetheless quite sharp. Her stern had been designed to accommodate steam propulsion, which was never fitted. Forward of the rudder there were two stern posts with a filled-in propeller aperture between them. This narrow addition to the run aft may well have added to her speed. She is credited with a one day's run of 340 miles and is reputed to have exceeded 300 miles a number of times. Her fastest time to Sydney was 73 days and her fastest to Melbourne 64 days, the latter only five days more than the record set by the *Thermopylae*.

She was originally rigged with skysails over single topgallants, but this lofty rig reduced her stability and the skysails were removed after the second voyage. In 1883 she was given double topgallants on the fore and main. Her lower masts were of iron, her topmasts and lower yards were of steel, and the remaining spars of wood.

The majority of *Sobraon*'s passengers were accommodated in staterooms for from two to four people. All passenger quarters were located in the tweendeck, which ran from bow to stern immediately below the main deck. Under Devitt & Moore ownership she had, beginning at the stern, 27 first class staterooms, fourteen second class staterooms, and 32 third class staterooms. Forward of

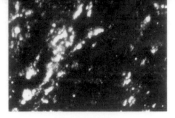

Sobraon

these there were two dormitories with rows of bunks for single men. The last twenty feet at the bow was taken up by a sail locker and a store room. Even with the tweendeck given over to passenger accommodation, she could still carry 3,200 tons of cargo in her lower hold.

Sobraon made only one round voyage each year, sailing from London in late September and from Australia in late February. This meant that she spent the summer in England. This easy schedule, and the good living conditions and food, made *Sobraon* very popular with the better class of seamen. Those who were fortunate enough to get a berth in her stayed year after year. Captain J. A. Elmslie took over the ship for her second voyage and remained in command until her seagoing career ended, 24 years later. James Cameron, a shipwright in the Alexander Hall yard, signed on as ship's carpenter in the original crew and held this post for all of her 25 voyages.

The food served on board rivalled, in its variety and quality, that of a hotel on shore. Much of it was prepared with meats and vegetables grown on the farm of Joseph Moore, the surviving partner of the shipowning firm (Thomas Henry Devitt had died in 1860). Moore had the produce and livestock delivered to the ship by his own farmhands all the way from the County of Cornwall in the far west of England.

BELOW LEFT: The *Sobraon's* figurehead, an elegant lady in an empire-line ballgown, was in keeping with the superior facilities, comfort and elegance on board.

BELOW RIGHT: At the helm of the *Sobraon.*

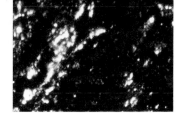

Perishable food could be stored in an icebox capable of holding ten tons of ice. The livestock for a typical voyage consisted of three milk cows, three bullocks, 90 sheep, 50 pigs, and 300 geese, chickens, ducks, and turkeys. The animals were housed in pens on deck between the hatches and deckhouses, and on top of the deckhouses between the ship's boats. Some of the chickens lived in coops under the benches built onto the sides of skylights and companionways for the relaxation of the passengers. Bales of fodder for the animals, also produced on the farm in Cornwall, took up further space on top of the deckhouses.

The ship's bell.

Christmas dinner on the ship, outward bound in 1890, consisted of: mock turtle soup, mutton cutlets "a la Reform," stewed oysters, curried prawns, Oxford sausages, jugged hare and jelly, cutlets "a la Prince de Galles," curried eggs, stuffed roast duck, boiled ham and sauce piquante, roast haunch of mutton and jelly, corned leg of pork and peas pudding, green peas, French beans, mashed and baked potatoes, plum pudding, mince pies, gooseberry meringue, trifles, and jellies.

One passenger noted in his diary: "6 p.m. Christmas Dinner and a capital one too. The men dressed for dinner and the ladies came out in their smart frocks. The dinner was excellent when one considers that we have now been out from London eleven weeks all but one day, and ten weeks and two days from Plymouth. No roast beef but a capital haunch of mutton. I proposed the Captain's health — a task which gave me great pleasure."

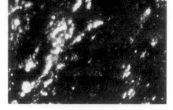

Sobraon

An engraving of the *Sobraon* at sea
on one of her voyages to Australia.

Sobraon enjoyed a reputation as a steady and dry ship. Even in strong gales very little water was taken over the main deck. She made her consistently fast passages without being driven hard. Captain Elmslie could have carried sail to the limit in the roaring forties, and by so doing might well have set new records, but the comfort of the passengers was more important.

Travellers bound for Australia in the late Victorian era were quite resourceful in finding ways to entertain themselves when conditions were favorable. On *Sobraon*'s voyage home in 1882 weekly dances were organized with music provided on the piano. On deck, quoits were played in the morning and cricket matches in the afternoon, the latter pitting passengers against the ship's officers and midshipmen. Concerts were given in the saloon and musical plays were performed. There was a Shakespeare Society, which gave readings, and a debating society. Among the questions debated in 1882 was, "The reading of the bulk of modern fiction is mentally and morally dangerous." The opposing viewpoint argued that novel reading was better than no reading and, " . . . far from being mentally and morally dangerous, it kept young people from doing worse."

The passengers were also entertained by traditional sailing ship rites of passage, performed by the crew. On *Sobraon*, as on many British ships, an elaborate ritual celebrated "burying the dead horse." Seamen were given an advance on their wages which was usually spent the last time ashore, or used to pay debts. The period at the start of the voyage was known as "working the dead horse." The traditional ceremony took place when this period had passed and wages again began to be earned.

Sobraon

1 0 3

Crewmen on the *Sobraon* in her early days repair rigging while a well-to-do passenger looks on.

An effigy of a horse was constructed of scraps of wood, and canvas stuffed with straw and painted. It was ridden about the deck by the youngest seaman while the rest of the crew sang the dead horse shanty. Then it was hoisted up to a yardarm and cut loose to drop into the sea, accompanied by the singing of "Rule Britannia" and a chorus of three cheers for the captain. On *Sobraon*'s outward voyage in 1882 the following announcement of the dead horse ceremony was posted:

By kind permission of Captain Elmslie a grand procession of the "Dead Horse" will take place on Wednesday evening, 18th October at 7:15 p.m. on the upper deck. Order of Procession: 1st. Two constables. 2nd. The jockey on the horse, accompanied by his wife. 3rd. 18 seamen two by two. 4th. The horse will stop at the quarter deck to be viewed by the passengers (ladies are requested to give him plenty of room as he is liable to kick). The procession will then move on slowly. 5th. The sale of the Horse. 6th. Thrilling death and burial of the Horse. 7th. Conclude with a concert. The general company are respectfully invited. Carriages may be ordered for 10:30 p.m. God Save the Queen.

A sunny picture of the *Sobraon*'s crew during a cruise.

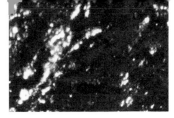

Changing sail in the tropics.

There were two welcome breaks on each homeward voyage. About six weeks after the ship left Melbourne a stop was made at Cape Town. Some cargo and supplies were taken aboard, and the passengers had time ashore for shopping and sightseeing. About two weeks after leaving Cape Town the ship called at Jamestown on the Island of St Helena. The popular excursion here was a climb to the 1,800-foot-high plateau above the town to see the house where Napoleon had lived in exile, and the tomb where his body had been interred until it was returned to France in 1840. Often, in the evening, the musical or dramatic groups from the ship provided entertainment for the local people.

Sobraon's career was remarkably free of serious incidents. There was the inevitable rigging damage in severe gales, but no major dismasting. There were at least two fatal falls from aloft, and two miraculous survivals. One seaman fell from the main upper topsail yard onto the main lower shrouds, where he broke seven of the ratlines spread across them as footholds. The ratlines in turn broke his fall so that he landed on the rail virtually uninjured. Another man

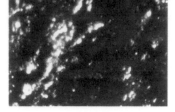

Sobraon

The boys from the *Sobraon* at play in Snails Bay, Balmain, in Sydney Harbor.

fell from the main yard 58 feet above the deck. He gathered himself up into a ball, covering his head with his arms; he suffered so little injury that within a month he had fully recovered.

A young woman, apparently a suicide, went overboard from the stern in November 1883 somewhere in the southern hemisphere. It was a dark night and the seas were high, and although a boat was launched within four minutes, she was not found. An apprentice accidentally fell overboard in the tropics one morning. He was a good swimmer, and was able to survive until the ship had been stopped and a boat sent back for him.

Sobraon's last voyage out to Australia was completed on 4 January 1891. There were 80 passengers on board. After passengers and cargo were discharged at Melbourne, the ship was sold to the government of New South Wales for £12,500. She was towed to Sydney, converted to a floating reformatory for boys, and anchored in the harbor off Cockatoo Island, a naval dockyard. She replaced the hulk *Vernon*, which had served in this capacity since 1867.

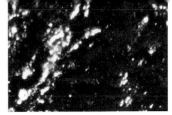

The boys of the **Sobraon** *spectacularly demonstrate one of the skills they learned on their floating reformatory, while the ship was moored off Cockatoo Island in Sydney Harbor from 1891 to 1911. The ship became home, school and training centre for boys whose parents had turned to crime or who had committed minor offenses themselves. To aid discipline they were dressed in sailors' uniforms and caps, and encouraged to take part in exercises like the one photographed here.*

The offenses for which the boys were sent to the ship tended to be minor ones. Many were guilty only of vagrancy, or were being taken away from poor parents who had been arrested. The ship was intended to remove them from the temptation to engage in crime, while giving them a general education and training in useful skills. Many recreational activities were also provided, including cricket, football, swimming, and band. Sports facilities on Cockatoo Island were made available to the school. The band became proficient enough to participate in public ceremonies and made several tours of the state of New South Wales.

In 1911 the shipboard reformatory was replaced by more modern facilities ashore. The Australian Government decided to acquire the *Sobraon* and use her as a stationary training ship for the new Royal Australian Navy. Her rig was further reduced to one yard on each mast, she was painted a lighter color, moved to a new anchorage in Rose Bay, Sydney, and renamed HMAS *Tingira*, an Australian Aboriginal name meaning "open sea" or "open water." In this capacity the ship trained another 3,158 Australian boys before it was retired in 1927.

The old *Sobraon* had by now been a fixture in Sydney Harbour for more than 35 years, and had played a part in the lives of many Australians. It was hoped that she might be preserved as some sort of naval or maritime museum, but this did not happen. Much of her teak planking was in good enough condition to be put to further use, and her iron frames had value as scrap. She was grounded in shallow water and largely broken up during the 1930s. Some remnants of her lower hull could still be seen there decades later.

The valiant *Sobraon* reaches the end of her days.

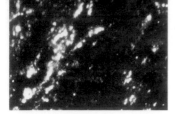

ACKNOWLEDGEMENTS

The Publisher would like to thank the following for contributing photographs to this publication.

British Museum, London 8, 9, 10, 11, 12, 13, 14, 15

City of Portsmouth Museum 30-1, 39

Colin Martin 35

Mary Rose Trust, Portsmouth 27, 32, 33, 34, 36, 38

Museum of the City of New York 86

National Portrait Gallery, London 27, 37

National Maritime Museum, Greenwich 2, 50, 51, 52, 53, 54, 57, 58, 59, 88, 94

Pepys Library, Magdalene College, Cambridge 28-9

Royal Naval Museum, Portsmouth 55

South Street Seaport Museum, New York 93

State Library of New South Wales, Sydney 96, 100-1 (by kind permission of Rodney Allcot, representing the Allcot Trust) 102, 107

Sydney Maritime Museum 74, 76, 77, 78-9, 80, 81, 82, 83, 84, 85, 89, 91, 98, 103, 104, 105, 106, 108

West Australian Museum, Fremantle 62, 63, 64, 65, 66, 67, 68, 69, 70, 71, 72, 73

Vasamuseet, Stockholm 25, 40, 42-3, 44, 45, 46, 47, 48, 49

Viking Ship Museum (Universitet i Oslo) 7, 16, 17, 18, 19, 20, 21, 23

INDEX

Italic page numbers refer to illustrations.

A

Agamemnon 53
American clippers 75
ammunition 55, *57*
Anglo-Saxon period 7
   Sutton Hoo 9–15
archers 33, 36
Armada 41, 48
artillery *see* guns
Asa, Queen 20
Australia 64, 69, 83, 84, 106

B

Baker, Matthew 41
Barak, Adrian *34*
barber-surgeon's cabin, *Mary Rose 32*, 33
barks 87–8
barrows *see* burials
Bastard Culverin *27*
Batavia 63–73, *65–73*
Battle of Trafalgar *51*, 51–6, *54*
Beagle 72
bell of the *Sobraon 99*
Beowulf (poem) 10
boots from the Oseberg ship *18*
Bordes (Anton) et Fils 87–8
Brighton 94–5
British East India Company 61
broadside *47*
Brouwer, Hendrik 64, 66
Brown, Basil 12–14
Bucentaure 55
buckets
   Oseberg ship 7, *21*
   Sutton Hoo 15, *21*
buckle from Sutton Hoo 9, *9*, *14*
"Buddha bucket" *7*, *21*
building techniques *see* construction
Bulmer, Ian 46
burials 6–7
   Oseberg ship 19–22
   Sutton Hoo 9–10
"burying the dead horse" 102–4

C

Cairngorm 75
Cameron, James 98
Campbell, George 85
cannons *see* guns
Cape Town 105
Captain 53
Carew, Sir George 27
cargo loading ritual 92
cargo ships *see* clippers
Carl 87
Carr, Frank 85
cart from the Oseberg ship 20, *21* carvings
   Oseberg ship 7, *17*, *18*, 19
   Wasa 44, 44–5, *46*, *48–9*
castleworks 34
cauldrons
   Oseberg ship *20*
   Sutton Hoo 10
Cheops 6
Chile 91–2
Christianity, conversion to 10
Christmas dinner on the *Sobraon* 99
clinker technique 17, 60
clipper ships 61
   Batavia 63–73, *65–73*
   Cutty Sark 74, 75–85, *76–8*, *82–5*
clothing
   Oseberg ship *18*
   Sutton Hoo 9–10
Cockatoo Island 106–8, *107*
coins
   Batavia 66
   Sutton Hoo 10, *14*
Collingwood, Vice-Admiral Cuthbert 54
color of the *Preussen* 90
compass *32*
construction
   Mary Rose 33–6, *35*
   Oseberg ship 17, 17–19
   Preussen 89–90
   Sobraon 97
   Sovereign 34
   Sutton Hoo *11*, 15
   Victory 53, 56–9
   Wasa 45, *45*

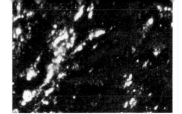

C (continued)

cooking implements
Oseberg ship *20*
Sutton Hoo 10
Cornelisz, Jeronimus 66, 69–72
Cutty Sark 74, 75–85, 76–80, 82–5

D

Deane, Charles 31
Deane, John 31
deck
Elizabethan period 34
Preussen 89
decorations *see* carvings
Devitt & Moore 97
Dowman, Captain Wildred 85
Drake-Brockman, Henrietta 72
dugout canoes 60
Dutch East India Company 60, *62*, 63

E

East Indies 63–4
Egerton, Professor Harold 32
Egypt 6
Elephant 53
Elizabethan period 41–3
Elmslie, Captain J. A. 98, 102
excavation
Batavia 73
Mary Rose 32–3, *33*, 35
Oseberg ship 19, *19*
Sutton Hoo 12–15
Wasa 46–8

F

Ferreira 85
figurehead
Cutty Sark 77
Oseberg ship *18*, 19
Sobraon 98
Victory 58
Wasa 44, *44*
food
Sobraon 99
Victory 59
Fougaux 55

F (continued)

France 87
Franzen, Anders 47
funeral ceremonies, Viking 22

G

grave-robbers
Oseberg ship 22–3
Sutton Hoo 12
graves *see* burials
gun decks on the *Wasa* 48
gunports on the *Wasa* 47
guns
see also ammunition
development 24–5
fifteenth century 34
sixteenth century 41
Batavia 72
Mary Rose 27, 36–8, *39*
Wasa 44, *44*, 47, 48
Gustafson, Gabriel 19
Gustavus Adolphus, King of Sweden 44

H

Hall (Alexander) & Co 75, 97
Hartog, Dirk 64
hat from the *Wasa 44*
Hays, Wiebe 71
helmet from Sutton Hoo *8*, 9
Henry VIII, King of England *26*, 27, *37*
Henry Grace a Dieu 27
Houtman, Frederick 64
Houtman's Abrolhos 64, 68
hulks 106
Hybertsson, Henrik 44, 46

I

Industrial Revolution 61
Invereshie 75
iron hulls 61, 87

J

Jacobs, John 12
Jacobsz, Ariaen 66–9
Japan 92–3
Java *63*, 64
Jonsson, Erik 46

J (continued)

jute trade 83

K

kerosene trade 83, 92
king buried at Sutton Hoo 9–10

L

Laeisz, Ferdinand B. 87, 89
Leviathan 55
life at sea
Cutty Sark 81, 84
Napoleonic period 56, *58*, 58–9
Sobraon 98–104
Linton, Hercules 75
livestock 99
longbow *34*
Lucas, Jean-Jacques 55
lyre from Sutton Hoo 10, *10*

M

McKee, Alexander 32
Maria do Amparo 85
Mary Rose 27–36, *27–38*, *38–9*
mascot 19
massacre of the *Batavia* 70–1
Moodie, Captain George 80–2, *82*
Moore, Captain F. W. 83
Moore, Joseph 98
mutiny on the *Batavia* 67–72, *70–1*
Mylen, Lucretia van der 67, 72

N

National Maritime Museum 85
National Maritime Trust 85
Navigation Acts repealed 75
Nelson, Lord 38, 51–6, *53*
Neptune 55
Netherlands 63–4
New York Harbor *93*
Nissen, Captain J. Hinrich 94–6
nitrate trade 91–3

O

Oriental 75
Oseberg ship *16–23*, *17–23*
ownership of Sutton Hoo site 14

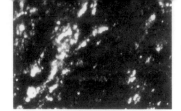

Index

P

paganism
    burial rites 6, 9–10
    Viking funeral 22
Pascoe, Lieutenant Crawford 72
passenger liner *Sobraon* 97–108
Peckell, Andreas 46
Pelsaert, Francis 66–70
Peter Pomegranite 35
Petersen, Captain Boye 93–4
Phillips, Charles 14–15
planks
    development 60
    Oseberg ship 12–23, *17*
Portugal 63
Postosi 88
powder monkeys 51
Pretty, Edith 12, 14
Preussen 86, 87–95, 88–92, 94
Punjaub 76
purse from Sutton Hoo 9–10, *12, 14*
pyre 22

Q

queen buried in Oseberg ship 20–3

R

race of clippers 80–2, *82*
Raedwald, king of the East Angles 9–10
Redoutable 55
reformatory 106–8
rigging
    iron ships 87
    Mary Rose 34
    Preussen 91
    Sobraon 97
    square 60
    three-masted 25
    Wasa 45
roof decoration of the *Wasa* 46
rowing vesels
    Oseberg ship *16–23*, 17–23
    Sutton Hoo *8–15*, 9–15
royal burials 9–10, 20–3
Royal Sovereign 54
rudder of the *Cutty Sark* 81–2, *82, 85*
Rule, Dr Margaret 32

S

sails
    development 60
    iron ships 87
St Helena 105
salvage operations *see* excavation
Santa Ana 54
Santissima Trinidad 55
Scotland 6, 77, 80
Scott & Linton (firm) 77
Scottish Maid 75
sculpture *see* carvings
servants slain 20–2
shield from Sutton Hoo 9, *15*
shipbuilding *see* construction
shipwreck
    Batavia 68–9
    Preussen 94, 94–5
shoe from the *Mary Rose 32*
shoulder clasps from Sutton Hoo 9, *12*
silverware from Sutton Hoo 10, *13*
sinking
    also shipwreck
    Mary Rose 27–30, *30*
    Wasa 46
Slade, Sir Thomas 53
Sobraon 96, 97–108, *98–108*
sodium nitrate trade 87
Souza, Captain 85
Sovereign 34
Spooner, William 12
spoons from Sutton Hoo 10, *13*
square rigging 60
Standard Oil Company 92
steam engines 61
steel 61
Stornoway 75
strakes 17
Sutton Hoo *8–15*, 9–15
sword from Sutton Hoo 9
Sydney Harbour 108

T

tea trade 75, 80–1
Temeraire 55
Thames Nautical Training College 85
Thermopylae 81–2, 84

T (continued)

timber *see* planks
Tingira 108
Tiptaft, Captain W. E. 83
Trafalgar *51,* 51–6, *54*
Treileben, Albrecht von 46
troop carriers 24–5, 36
Tudor period 33–5
Tweed 76

V

Vanguard 53
Verenigde Oost-Indische Compagnie
    (Dutch East India Company) 60, *62,* 63
Victory 38, *50,* 51–9, *53–4, 59*
Viking period 7
    Oseberg ship *16–23,* 17–23
Viking Ship Museum 17
Villeneuve, Admiral 51

W

wagon 7
warships
    development 24–5
    Elizabethan period 41–3
    Mary Rose 27–36, 27–38, *38–9*
    Victory 50, 51–9, *53–4, 59*
    Wasa 40, 41–9, *42–9*
Wasa 40, 41–9, *42–9*
Waymouth, Bernard 75
weapons
    see also guns
    Sutton Hoo 9–10, *15*
    Viking *23*
whetstone from Sutton Hoo 9, *13*
Willis, John ("Jock") 75–8, 84
Willis, Robert 75–8, 81
Woodget, Captain Richard 84, *84*
wool trade 83, 84